RELIGIOUS EXPERIENCE: ITS NATURE AND FUNCTION IN THE HUMAN PSYCHE

RELIGIOUS EXPERIENCE: ITS NATURE AND FUNCTION IN THE HUMAN PSYCHE

The First John G. Finch Symposium on Psychology and Religion

———————————— *By* ————————————

WALTER HOUSTON CLARK, Ph.D.

H. NEWTON MALONY, Ph.D.

JAMES DAANE, Th.D.

ALAN R. TIPPETT, Ph.D.

With a Foreword by

Lee Edward Travis, Ph.D.

Dean, Graduate School of Psychology
Fuller Theological Seminary
Pasadena, California

CHARLES C THOMAS • PUBLISHER
Springfield • Illinois • U.S.A.

Published and Distributed Throughout the World by

CHARLES C THOMAS • PUBLISHER

Bannerstone House

301-327 East Lawrence Avenue, Springfield, Illinois, U.S.A.

© *1973, by* CHARLES C THOMAS • PUBLISHER

ISBN 0-398-02550-9

Library of Congress Catalog Card Number: 72-79185

AUTHORS

Walter Houston Clark, Ph.D.

Formerly Professor of the Psychology of Religion
Andover Newton Theological School
Newton Centre, Massachusetts

H. Newton Malony, Ph.D.

Associate Professor of Psychology
Graduate School of Psychology
Fuller Theological Seminary
Pasadena, California

James Daane, Th.D.

Professor of Pastoral Theology
Fuller Theological Seminary
Pasadena, California

Alan R. Tippett, Ph.D.

Professor of Anthropology
School of World Mission
Fuller Theological Seminary
Pasadena, California

FOREWORD

ABOUT ten years ago, John G. Finch recognized the need of a Christian dimension in the training of psychotherapists. He could not find a curriculum in the country that met his demands for this dimension. As a consequence, in a series of lectures at Fuller Theological Seminary, he proposed the establishment of a School of Psychology that would correlate theology and psychology in the preparation of clinical psychologists. There resulted after two or three years of study on his part, the opening of the Graduate School of Psychology in 1965.

From the beginning, in the classroom, in the hospital, and in the laboratory, always the thrust has been to relate theoretically and practically the disciplines of theology and psychology. As a token of appreciation to Dr. Finch for the conception of the school, the Seminary has designated a yearly discussion on psychology and religion to be known as the John G. Finch Symposium. The main idea of the Symposium is to pursue the conviction that the religious experience, so-called, is to be distinguished from a mundane experience. Many thoughtful students of psychology agree with this belief. And we will strive to provoke serious and hopefully penetrating consideration of the possibility.

The entire seminary family congratulates Dr. Malony for the successful inauguration of the Symposium. Much more lies in store for all of us.

LEE EDWARD TRAVIS

PREFACE

THE study of religious phenonema has been one of the foci of American psychology since the time of G. Stanley Hall. It has engaged the attention of many distinguished students. Its sluggish progress has probably been a function of the hesitancy of psychologists to invade sacrosanct areas, coupled with a lack of sustained experimental interest which would lead to adequate theoretical foundations.

Walter Houston Clark's efforts have been a welcome exception to the trend. His long-term involvement in the field led to the publishing of his *The Psychology of Religion* in 1958. The present essays could be conceived of as the integrating of themes from the 1958 volume with his more recent *Chemical Ecstacy: Psychedelic Drugs and Religion* (1969).

The emphasis on the nature and functioning of individual religious experience is of great contemporary interest. This book comes at a time when there is wide preoccupation with the meditative practices of Eastern religions along side of renewed vitality in more traditionally christian religious experiences, e.g. as seen in the Jesus-people movements. Further, there are explicit religious overtones to the public interest in encounter-group "peak" experiences.

The thrust of Clark's position is that man has the capacity for religious experience within himself. It is a potential that lies unused. His view is similar to that of William James. They both affirm a "gentle" mysticism which emphasizes the unique, life-changing quality of becoming aware of this dimension of life.

The most controversial aspect of the lectures is their affirmation of the value of induced religious experience through the use of drugs. Clark defends these procedures as legitimate triggers of genuine religious events.

The structure of the book allows for three responses to Clark's thesis. This greatly enriches the text, especially since a theologian and an anthropologist, in addition to another psychologist, respond. James Daane's penetrating critique of Clark's method from the viewpoint of Christian apologetics is of critical importance. Alan Tippett's more gentle acceptance of method is paralleled by his concern, as an anthropologist, with the experimental inducement condoned by Clark. These responses are matched by my own concern, as a psychologist, with Clark's easy willingness to separate religious from mundane experience. There are additional chapters which allow for a rebuttal by Clark and report the postlecture discussions.

I am indebted to the faculty and trustees of Fuller Theological Seminary whose vision made the John G. Finch Symposium on Psychology and Religion a possibility. President David Allan Hubbard nurtured the dream into a reality. I owe a continuing word of thanks to Dean Lee E. Travis and my colleagues in the Graduate School of Psychology for their support and direction. Their encouragement was the guiding force leading to this publication.

In an initial endeavor such as this, many persons help chart the course and bring a manuscript to press. I am especially grateful for the assistance of my secretaries, Marnie Frederickson and May Battany. Their help was invaluable.

Knowing that the field is moving rapidly, this volume is presented as a contribution to the history of the field. It is intended to be of special interest to theological and scientific scholars who are attempting to relate their disciplines. We can only hope that these essays provide dialogue and promote further thinking.

H. NEWTON MALONY

CONTENTS

RELIGIOUS EXPERIENCE:
ITS NATURE AND FUNCTION
IN THE HUMAN PSYCHE

And then with a resolution and cunning which one can hardly help admiring, men shut their eyes to that which is quite unique in the religious experience, even in its most primitive manifestations. But it is rather a matter for astonishment than for admiration! For if there be any single domain of human experience that presents us with something unmistakably specific and unique, peculiar to itself, assuredly it is that of the religious life.

−Rudolf Otto

Chapter 1

RELIGIOUS EXPERIENCE IN CONTEMPORARY PERSPECTIVE

WALTER HOUSTON CLARK

IN his great volume, *The Varieties of Religious Experience,* William James (1958, p. 2) quotes J. H. Leuba: "God is not known; he is not understood; he is used . . ." A great deal of the reading that I do, both in the psychological and religious area − maybe some of it my own − strikes me more designed to advance the reputation of the writers than in producing information to be used. We seem to be involved in a game called scholarship, where we score points by getting read. If you will forgive me the comparison with God, and though I never object to being read and understood, in these three lectures I hope most of all to be *used.*

In this first lecture, I intend to point out, in view of its crucial importance to religion, what I see as the shameful neglect of religious experience by psychological and religious scholars alike. Then I will review a few of the chief figures in the field and how they have treated their subject matter. I will take the somewhat unpopular position that religion, in its essence, is unique. This

3

should enable us to put our study in perspective and form a background for the following two lectures.

In the second lecture, I will describe and discuss the chief forms that religious experience takes, with an emphasis on mysticism. In the final lecture, I will point out the effects that these experiences can be expected to have on the experiencers. Here is where I expect that my lectures will be the most useful. I will try to present you with a rationale of religious experience, why it is desirable, and what we can expect it to do for us, as well as what we should *not* expect it to do. The whole approach, I suppose, could be called *phenomenonological,* if we need a long word for it.

RELIGIOUS EXPERIENCE IN THE CHURCH

Although religious experience is a universal phenomenon and the monopoly of no faith, for the most part I will have in mind Christian references and illustrations. This, I must confess, derives from my provincialism. I am a Christian and so better acquainted with the history of my own faith in which my roots are fixed. But this does not mean that I will not glance at other religions, nor that I intend a Christian apologetic. The latter is not my field, nor would it be appropriate to my task if it were. I am a social scientist, and any scientist is concerned with observing his field dispassionately and reporting what he sees there.

Just as there is no Hindu point of view in the study of physics or chemistry to be set against a Christian point of view, so, at least in the way I am approaching my field, there is not a Christian psychology of religion to be distinguished from any other. I am simply mentioning my bias, since, social science being the broad study that it is, you may be aware of it if I should stray from the straight and narrow path of scientific objectivity, as I expect that here and there I may do. On the other hand, if, to some of you, I do not seem to be Christian enough, I want you to be aware of how I conceive my task. I am not a student of Christian psychology but a psychologist who happens to be a Christian, and if I look for universal aspects of my field, I do not think that One who gave to us the parable of the Good Samaritan would find any objection in this.

If we look at the Judeo-Christian tradition, we can find many examples of the key importance of religious experience among religious leaders, beginning with Abraham and Moses, continuing through the prophets and coming to flower with special cogency in Jesus' baptism, his temptation, and the agony of Calvary. The shape of early Christianity was formed by the encounter with Christ by Saul of Tarsus on the Damascus Road, while an early form of Christian monastic community was that which spontaneously grew up around the figure of the visionary St. Anthony. Mysticism was a recurring phenomenon throughout the Church of the Middle Ages, and a large number of ecstatics of varying quality has continued until our own day.

The religious experiences of Martin Luther are well known, while it was the mystic George Fox who brought to a decadent England the emphasis on the spiritual search in the interior life and honesty in its exterior so needed in the seventeenth century. The next century saw the rise of Methodism based on the need for conversion required by that powerful religious figure John Wesley, following his own conversion. Allied with a pietism deriving from the Anabaptists of the continent, and fed on the Gospel accounts of Paul and the declaration by Jesus to Nicodemus that to be saved he must be born again, the Protestant churches of the last century, particularly in the United States, have emphasized conversion. Particularly for the Methodists, a conversion experience was a requisite for church membership, but recently there has been a loosening or even a total lapsing of this requirement, which Wesley would doubtless deplore were he to be suddenly materialized on the modern Methodist scene.

Similar relaxations have occurred in other evangelical churches, and despite such effective evangelists as Billy Sunday, Frank Buchman, and Billy Graham, evangelism and religious experience have not received the backing from theologians and church leaders that it had at the turn of the century. But the basic urges of human nature are not to be denied, and the longing for oneness and the inner encounter with God, the urge to plumb the mystery of life and the essential meaning of the cosmos have reappeared in what, to our respectable Christian eyes, seems a strange form in the interest of our young people in yoga, Zen, and other Eastern forms. Scholars have variously called this "the counterculture" or "the green rebellion." The "silent majority" has looked on such religious eruptions with suspicion and stigmatized practitioners as "hippies."

WHY HAS RELIGIOUS EXPERIENCE BEEN NEGLECTED?

While it would be a mistake to state that religious experience, particularly in the form of conversion in the evangelical churches, has been ignored, nevertheless, emphasis on it has fallen off since the last century, at least until very recently. The contemplative orders in the Catholic churches, superbly designed to nourish the mystical life, have greatly declined in numbers and influence since the Middle Ages. Even the Society of Friends, with its spiritual life based on the Inner Light, has moved in the direction of relatively more reliance on reason and social activism since the days of Fox. Correlatively, the Hasidic tradition, the nourishing soil of prophecy in Judaism, definitely occupies a minority position among Jews. With few exceptions, denominational leaders and religious intellectuals tend to put their emphasis on other aspects of religion than experience. What are some of the reasons for this neglect?

First of all, and particularly with respect to the evangelical lessening of stress on conversion, there is the ease with which conversion may be faked, or at least substituted for, by words of piety. I suppose every church can demonstrate the phenomenon. I can remember a woman in the church in which I grew up. Everyone in the church acknowledged that there was no more tireless worker − or talker − than Miss B., and no one nearer to God by her own confession. The only trouble was that nobody liked her and secretly hoped that if conversion had made her what she was, they would never experience it.

Furthermore, as with Miss B., what many Protestants claimed was a profound religious experience was often nothing more than a shallow emotionalism followed either by a rigid dogmatism or backsliding that left the worshipper in a worse state than before. Quite obviously, if a conversion were to be *required* as prerequisite to a desired membership in the Church, such events might be expected. Jesus reminded his followers that the wind of the spirit blows where it wills. Coercion creates a poor climate for religious experience, and Methodism was wise to drop the requirement, though not necessarily the emphasis.

A more subtle and more pervasive reason for neglect of experience is the Western emphasis on science and the faith that through reason, life can be controlled. Child of the European Enlightenment with its emphasis on reason and, more remotely, of the prominence given by the Medieval church to Aristotle with his interest in logic and science, Western culture has always emphasized reason and so given birth to contemporary science. This is opposed to Eastern culture with its greater emphasis on art and religious mysticism. It has meant that Western religion, as well as Western culture in general, has preferred form, institutional framework, moral law, dogma, and the theological thinking on which such things are based, to the uncertainties of ecstasy in any form.

This has led in our seminaries, where church leadership is forged, to a kind of academic class consciousness. So complete in its conquest over the loyalties of the best student minds is science that it is science that wins the lion's share of academic rewards. It is understandable that unconsciously, many a seminary professor has felt like a poor relation of his university counterpart whose salary is so much higher than his. In his zeal to prove that his brain is as big as one possessed by a scientist, he imitates the scientist in emphasizing the rigor of his logical thought processes. In so doing, he runs the danger of neglecting the ecstasy that is not only the source of prophetic fire but the gateway into that which supports his own faith. It is faith which constitutes the roots of civilization and even may save science from itself.

A third reason for the neglect of religious experience we might call the "cult of privacy." The unwillingness to wear one's heart on one's sleeve derives largely from two sources — shame and fear. But both derive basically from the unwillingness to be vulnerable, to show to the world inner aspects of our personalities whether we are ashamed of them or because they are too precious to us to risk their being laughed at or misunderstood. In the latter category are many profound and poignant religious experiences. I have known more than one student to confess to me ecstatic experiences so precious to them that they had never been confided to anyone before. They were told to me only after the students felt sure that I would keep their confidences and not belittle them.

The second source of the cult of privacy is the genuine fear all of us have of our unconscious urges. Even though we sense that they are the sources of our highest capacities, we fear that anything so powerful may get out of hand. These could either destroy us by plunging us into an uncontrollable chaos or require of us a life style so radical that we would be unwilling to accept it. We remember here the story of Jesus and the rich young ruler. And how many of us, no matter how fond we are of reading the gospel story, are willing to leave all and follow Him? Indeed our churches themselves are not willing to risk anything so revolutionary, for there is nothing which the churches fear quite so much as they do religion!

The somewhat contradictory fourth reason for the rejection of religious experience is probably the most creditable. This is the desire for a life of active righteousness. There is so much that is wrong with the world; so many rights that are violated; so much strife, poverty, and unnecessary suffering that it seems self-centered to wallow in the enjoyments of religious experience and leave such tasks undone. There is much to be said for this point of view and not much to be said for religious experience, unless it can be demonstrated that the good life, the fruits of righteousness, does indeed come from such a source.

THE FUNCTION OF THE NONRATIONAL
IN RELIGIOUS EXPERIENCE

The intellect is not enough. Those who wish to cope with the problems and complexities, the human resistance and wilfulness, both within themselves and outside of themselves, require a factor of far greater strength than merely *seeing* the path through the spectacles of reason. This factor is to be found within religion, but religion of a far more dynamic and passionate nature than that presented to us by our religious intellectuals. And it is my belief that only this type of religion offers the slightest promise of winning for us the war against universal greed, suspicious hate, and lust for power. Its central characteristic must be strength, just as its chief flower is compassion and love.

This does not mean that intelligence and reason should have no role in religion. Their role is indeed most important. It is only that reason has been overemphasized as the means through which we approach God and control our behavior. But I must clarify its function by setting it over against what Rudolf Otto calls the "non-rational factor" in religion, and what Schleiermacher would call "feeling."

But first I must make clear that what I am talking about is not the *irrational*. True, this nonrational component of religious experience may *become* irrational if not directed at least in part by the rational. But through the day we engage in many activities of a nonrational nature that are not irrational. The delight that most of us take in listening to music, for example, is nonrational, but it is not irrational. Intuition is nonrational, but to be guided by our intuitions is not necessarily irrational.

The function of the nonrational in religious experience is to lend it liveliness, color, and energy. Otto points out that it is not merely fascinating but threatening and awesome as well. It is the *mysterium tremendum* or "the mystery that makes one tremble." It is no light thing to be grasped by the power of this mystery. It was the sense of this power that made Moses take off his shoes before the burning bush. It helps us to understand the writer of Hebrews when he said, "It is a fearful thing to fall into the hands of the living God" (Heb. 10:31). Weak people reject this power and keep it at arm's length by staying within rules and watering it down through a comforting theology. Or, being grasped by it, they may lose their nerve and retreat into madness or the comforting familiarity of the commonplace. The adventurous searcher will seek it even while he fears it, and through this courage will discover the strength that characterizes all effective religion.

Otto (1958, p. 46) likens the religious life to a piece of cloth with the rational interpenetrating the nonrational as the warp of the cloth interpenetrates the woof. The function of the rational is to guide, direct, and criticize the nonrational. The two might be compared to the engine and the rudder of a ship. The rudder directs the ship and the engine makes it go. With no matter how accurate a rudder, the ship will lie still in the water and get nowhere. With a powerful engine alone, the ship will become a danger to itself and other navigation. Each part needs the other. And so it is with the rational and the nonrational in religion.

In one of his perceptive poems, Robert Frost mentions the two theories of the end of the world, through fire or freezing cold. He says

> . . . for destruction ice
> Is also great and would
> suffice.

Through his allegory, he could have been speaking of religion, where the fire of ecstasy, which sustains both poetry and religion, if unchecked, may consume both poet and prophet. The religious fanatic is one religious form of this misfortune. This is just one example of the nonrational getting out of hand.

But just as lethal, the much more present danger to Western faith is the suffocating effects of intellectual ice and the overemphasis on the rational. The young pastor fresh from the seminary, for example, tries to feed his congregation a diet of sermons taken from his professors' lectures. Here and there a church puts its financial foundations on the line by taking a stand against social injustice and war. Nevertheless, on the whole, church programs tend to be harmless and bland. Often they do not go very far beyond what any Rotary Club or fraternal organization might promote.

Instead of the vigorous spiritual life that might be expected within the churches, the nonrational is represented mostly through the participation of a fraction of the congregation in the singing of two or three traditional hymns or, in the wealthier churches, through the listening to an anthem sung impeccably by a paid choir. This anemic emotionalism is sometimes supplemented through the preaching of a visiting evangelist whose words either fall on deaf ears or promote conversions from which backsliding frequently occurs. Otherwise, especially in the upper-middle-class churches, sermons demonstrate the intellectual class consciousness I previously referred to in connection with seminaries, particularly when congregations are largely college bred. With such emphases, the church organization takes on greater and greater significance, based on theology and dogma that have derived more from tradition and cold intellectual interchange than on a living encounter with God. The power that originally brought these churches into being has largely been forgotten.

Such things as roots in honored tradition and the play of keen minds are very much to be desired in the church. It is when the rational spirit loses touch with the nonrational that the ice of intellectualism and the hollow shell of institutional structure mark the decline of a dying religion.

On the other hand, what I wish to make clear is that it is the balance and harmonious interaction between rational and nonrational that keeps a religion alive. Since both institutions and individuals grow, and times change, this balance changes with the needs of the times. Consequently, there is no fixed formula that, put into the hands either of organizations or individuals, can serve as a prescription to be relied on to guide us in every detail. It is easy to look back into history and find institutions that weakened or even destroyed themselves by overemphasizing dogma, tradition, or a set of moralistic rules, and also by the reverse.

For this reason, religion can never become a science, a technique for each person to follow, no matter with what longing he may seek for such. Like the tightrope walker's art, the pilgrim's progress is an art, first bending to this side, then to that, so that the perils on both sides of this straight and narrow way may be negotiated. The outlines of the Celestial City gleam and then gloom before the pilgrim's eye. Rudolf Otto (1958, p. 41-142) in *The Idea of The Holy* sums up my point gracefully:

> By the continual living activity of its non-rational elements a religion is guarded from passing into 'rationalism.' By being steeped in and saturated with rational elements it is guarded against sinking into fanaticism or mere mysticality, or at least from persisting in these, and is qualified to become a religion for all civilized humanity. The degree in which both rational and nonrational elements are jointly present, united in healthy and lovely harmony, affords a criterion to measure the relative rank of religions — and one, too, which is specifically religious.

IS RELIGION UNIQUE?

Against this background, I think you are in a better position to understand what I mean by religion, though I must admit that defining religion is no easy talk. Any unabridged dictionary will list 10 or 15 different definitions, while each person discussing or even studying the subject will likely have a definition as unique as his way of writing his signature (cf. Clark, 1958, pp. 17-28). But there are families of definitions and trends as one age gives way to another.

A strong recent trend among religious scholars and social scientific students of religion is to make religion inclusive or, in other words, secularize it, as in Harvey Cox's *The Secular City*. A man's religion is expressed in everything that he does, in all the thoughts he thinks, and in all of his relationships. There is a profound truth in this conception, and for some purposes it may be very useful. However, despite my warning against the fallacy of reductionism which I plan for you in the next lecture, I believe that it is possible to reduce religion to an essential principle, namely *the inner experience of the Holy*. This experience grows out of mystical states of consciousness. If it is present, then we have religion, at least in embryo. If it is absent, then religion exists only in a truncated, attenuated form. In an article in *Lumen Vitae* several years ago, I suggested mysticism as a basic concept in defining the religious self (Clark, 1964).

But this does not mean that the experience of the Holy should not in some way overspread and touch all of life, as it surely will if it is vigorous. In a certain sense, the psychology of religion is the same as the psychology of anything else, as William James points out. But he also notes that in mysticism, we have the root of personal religious experience, and certainly in the mystical forms of consciousness we have a condition that differs radically from other forms of the everyday waking state (James, 1958). But it is from this germ that religious societies spring with their attendant theologies, institutional forms, celebrations, saints, prophets, moral codes, sense of obligations to others and to society, meditations, pangs of conscience, and activities.

In a secondary or even tertiary sense, we might admit certain activities to be religious (cf. Clark, 1958, pp. 23-28). The administration of a church's finances, for example, might be defined as religious activity, though a very good job could be done by a banker by exactly the same principles and perhaps very similar motivations as those by which he runs his bank. A crusade for peace sponsored by a church might be participated in not because the participants loved their enemies but because of generalized idealism galvanized by charismatic but not necessarily religious leaders. Indeed some who advocate peace in the name of Christianity display a violence of animosity toward any who disagree with them that calls in question their capacity to love their neighbors, let alone their enemies. Such persons require the compassion that is generated by religious experience as I am defining it, and the gentling influence that comes from a confrontation with the Christ of the Gospels.

If secularized religion means the bringing to such activities the warmth and compassion that results from an experience of brotherhood associated with the sense of the Holy, then such religion remains religion of a very high order. But if secularization means the gradual loss of this essential religious attitude, as so often it does, then this will mark progressive religious impoverishment. Thus every act or attitude may or may not have its religious component, and the religious component, in principle, can be distinguished from it. Like heat, of which every tangible object may have its share or lack, but which can be distinguished from the object itself, so with religion. Much in life that passes for religion is cold for the lack of it.

The difference between the secular and religious perception of a creature, for example, may be illustrated by the typically Western and Eastern attitudes toward a poisonous snake, say a cobra. On seeing the snake the typical Western reaction is not only to abhor the snake, run from it, or, if means are available, destroy the malevolent creature. But the pious Buddhist or Hindu sees the snake differently. He knows of course the dangers of contact with the snake, that it may kill him and his children too. Yet so great is his reverence for life that he allows the cobra to nest beneath his house. This attitude may be due simply to what his fathers and his priests have taught him, in which case we can call it religious only in a very indirect sense. It is only a little removed in a religious direction from the secularized attitude of the typical Westerner, which has nothing of the religious about it, unless of a negative variety.

But if our pious Indian has been informed by a profound mystical experience, he will then see the cobra as a fellow creature, an object of fascination and beauty. Like the grass under his feet, the clear water that he drinks, the bright sun that warms him, or the mists that wrap him around, the cobra becomes another jeweled expression of the cosmos and another expression of the cunning workmanship of his Maker. Therefore, though with fear and with dread yet with fascination and with reverence, he will protect this enemy turned friend. He knows that, unlike his own kind, the creature will not seek him out to destroy him but will attack only if it sees its own safety in question. Thus the two live in mutual peace, a peace guaranteed by the essential religious nature of the Indian.

Thus my answer to the question Is religion unique? is an unqualified *yes*. Though religion can permeate every act and attitude of man, essentially it derives from man's living and immediate encounter with the Holy, the fruit of mysticism.

THE STUDY OF RELIGIOUS EXPERIENCE

Historical

Malony (1970) recently read an excellent paper on "New Methods in the Psychology of Religion" at the annual meeting of the Society for the Scientific Study of Religion. In the paper, he spoke of the importance for the student of religion to have had some firsthand experience of his subject matter. It used to be the idea that any self-respecting scientist should be careful never to involve himself in the medium he was studying, and this may be another reason why scholars of religion have often felt themselves to be second-class citizens in the academic world.

But in recent years, science itself has devised a method – or perhaps simply recognized it – in what was christened in 1940 as "participant observation" by the sociologist Florence Kluckhohn (1940, pp. 331-343). Some form of participant observation leading to an empathic understanding of their subject matter has characterized all of the leading students of psychology of religion in the past and is likely to have been the reason for many of us, like myself, taking up the field at all.

In America, the true pioneer was G. Stanley Hall, a man of broad experience and education, who shocked Boston in the early 1880's by studying adolescents and suggesting that conversion was an adolescent phenomenon. Hall also started *The Journal of Religious Psychology,* published from 1904 to 1915, and hopefully soon to be re-established. The first book entitled *The Psychology of Religion*, was published by a student of Hall, Edwin Diller Starbuck, in 1899. This was followed in 1902 by what is still the most eminent book on the subject, *The Varieties of Religious Experience,* by William James. Not only religiously and psychologically perceptive, it focuses on the religion of the individual. The book is lively and well written, permeated as it is with the personality of this winsome philosopher. It is still read and represented in America alone by four or five separate editions still in print. Quite likely it will prove to be the most widely influential book on religion written anywhere in the Western world during the twentieth century.

Another author in the tradition of James was James B. Pratt, whose volume, *The Religious Consciousness* (1920), is perhaps second only to James in its penetrating view of religion. But the reputation of Pratt in his day was rivaled by that of George A. Coe. One of the reasons that the psychology of religion is not beloved by the typical psychologist is that it is difficult to do experiments with it. Animals seem not to have religious experience, and human beings get understandably touchy when they feel that their religious experience is being manipulated. But Coe was a pioneer in this field. By hypnotizing his subjects, he demonstrated that religious experience is a little more apt to come to those who are suggestible — at least among those who attend evangelistic meetings. Coe is also said to have rigged attendants at communion services with galvanometers and other indicators of physiological conditions in order to study their reactions.

However, by far the most popular, though very fallible, means of systematically studying religious experience in those days, as in this, was the questionnarie, or variations on it (cf. Clark, 1958, Chap. 3). A more up-to-date survey will be found in the papers of the Symposium on Methodology in the Psychology of Religion at the Scientific Study of Religion (1970).

After a lapse of about 30 years, due largely to the ascendency of behaviorism and an unspiritual Freudianism, interest in religion by psychologists began to have a modest revival in the 1950's. The two chief texts in the field to emphasize religious experience were my *The Psychology of Religion* (1958) and the second edition of Paul E. Johnson's *Psychology of Religion* (1959). I had been impressed by my reading of Pratt and James while in college, and doubtless my volume pays them the compliment of imitation. Johnson's book is in the same general tradition, though perhaps with not quite the emphasis on mysticism. The works of Orlo Strunk, Jr. (1959, 1962) also emphasize religious experience as well as concepts of the religious self.

All of these works show the influence of Gordon Allport's *The Individual and His Religion* (1950) and his *Becoming* (1955). In the latter volume, he developed his concept of the "proprium," a term derived from Swedenborg and touched with William James' concept of religion as an "acute fever" rather than a dull habit. What Allport is speaking of is the luminous core of personality which must be central in the individual's life, whatever his concerns, religious or nonreligious. Allport later developed his distinction between "intrinsic" and "extrinsic" religion, the former being more closely associated with religious values (Allport and Ross, 1967). Even Paul Pruyser who repudiates religious experience as a too-narrow concept for the psychologist of religion (e.g. Pruyser, 1968, pp. 4-5) and allows himself to range freely among varying aspects of the religious life, ends his volume with a definition of religion that makes principal use of the great proponents of religious experience, Schleiermacher, Otto, and William James.

Most other psychologists who have recently written on the psychology of religion have not emphasized religious experience. However, Evelyn Underhill, a mystic herself, published her distinguished work, *Mysticism,* in 1930. This is in part psychological and is still read and is influential. The late W. T. Stace in 1960 published a more closely reasoned and systematic study of the same subject in *Mysticism and Philosophy,* while Marghanita Laski published an original study in England in 1961 called

Ecstasy. I will return to all three of these authors in my next lecture.

In completely different traditions are two authors. One, Rodney Stark, is a sociologist who has categorized differing types of religious experience (1965, pp. 97-116). The other is the English psychiatrist William Sargant. In *The Battle for the Mind,* he has started with the unpromising field of Pavlovian psychology and research with references to war neuroses and brainwashing. Yet he has come up with a fascinating, readable, and suggestive study of religion that is far from being the uncomplimentary treatise on religious experience that one might expect. Yet it could be complained that he tends to produce a Procrustian bed into which he fits the various movements he studies.

Psychedelic Drugs

In the early years of the 1960's, certain religious scholars began to be aware of a superlative instrument for the study of religious experience. This was the psychedelic or "mind-revealing" drugs. They are mind revealing in the sense that people who ingest them nearly always become aware of capacities they did not know they possessed, the most surprising being their mystical potentialities. I have written about this subject in my *Chemical Ecstasy* (1969). Some self-styled experts have labeled the religious effects of the drugs illusory, a kind of religious fake. I have carefully and critically studied the subject for 10 years through firsthand investigation and self-experimentation and have come to the conclusion that if this is fake religion, then the fake is frequently better than the real thing. There are many well-attested cases on record of dramatic, lasting conversions and religious growth of a profound nature following use of LSD-type drugs.

The study of the religious agency of the drugs, at least in America, was initiated chiefly by Dr. Timothy Leary at Harvard, who gave psilocybin to convicts. Most of these volunteers reported intense religious experiences. I have carefully followed up some of them and can substantiate Leary's contentions. One of Massachusetts' most dangerous criminals had a vision of Christ which, since that moment in 1962, has completely kept him from crime.

I have just completed a survey of 100 users of LSD-type drugs, randomly selected and many of them hippies, and 20 users of *Cannabis* drugs. All reported at least some of the elements of profound religious experience, though not all of these users could be said to have had the well integrated and clearly formed religious experience of the majority. Of the users of LSD-type drugs, 76 per cent reported experience of the Holy, 61 per cent to an intense degree; 78 per cent reported psychological rebirth; while 32 per cent reported that their experience of God had been "beyond anything ever experienced or even imagined." Only one wished he had not taken the drugs, while 77 per cent reported the significance of their experience as intense, and half of the sample rated its significance as "beyond anything ever experienced or imagined." A teaching fellow at the State University of New York stated that since his experience, he has found a greatly increased sensitivity to religious values with particular openness to the wisdom of the mystics.

Responses such as these help us to understand certain very resistant aspects of the counterculture and "the green rebellion" along with the commune movement (cf. Hedgepeth and Stock, 1970 and Houriet, 1971).

But to return to the value of the drugs to the study of religious experience, let me say something of what is the most rigorously controlled and clearest in its conclusions of all experiments with religious experience with which I am familiar. Dr. Walter N. Pahnke, in a doctoral study done at Harvard, 1964) gave 10 theological students psilocybin under double-blind conditions with another 10 receiving a placebo and then sent all 20 to a Good Friday service. Nine of the 10 experimental subjects reported some of the characteristics of mystical experience, while only one of the control group did so. The results were statistically significant to a very high degree at the .001 level of confidence (cf. Clark, 1969, pp. 77-80).

In various investigations, I have confirmed Pahnke's results. I have increased the depth of my understanding of religion, whether released by the psychedelics or otherwise, through interviews and the study of religious documents produced by users (cf. Huxley, 1963 and Metzner, 1968). Such studies have persuaded me that at the very least, the conservative statement is justified as follows: *In some situations and with some people, and especially when both subject and guide intend it, the psychedelic drugs release very profound religious experience of a mystical nature.*

SUMMARY

I have sought to discuss the importance of religious experience to religion and also remark on the decline of the emphasis on it both practically and in the writings of influential theologians and scholars. I have suggested that this is due to the influence of the scientific world view, with its emphasis on the importance of control, the cult of privacy, the fear of subjective religion, and the emphasis in religion on social activism. But religion has at least as much need for the energies that spring from the nonrational urges based in man's unconscious as for the rational faculty that directs these urges and keeps them under some measure of control. The essential principle of religious experience is the subjective encounter with the Holy. It is the source of the religious dynamic which will bring the other aspects of life into the orbit of religion too. This marks religion as unique.

The psychological study of religious experience is a relatively modern discipline, having been started by G. Stanley Hall, then received momentum through that excellent volume of William James (1958), *The Varieties of Religious Experience.* These men set a high standard of scholarship and also demonstrated that empathic knowledge of their field which has characterized most effective investigation and writing in the psychology of religion. After a lapse of about 30 years, during the reign of behaviorism and psychoanalysis when psychologists treated religion as an almost atavistic human function, interest in the field of religious experience after the manner of James began to revive in the 1950's, with volumes by Allport, Clark, Johnson, and Strunk. Specialized contributions to knowledge of mysticism and conversion have been provided by works of Stace, Underhill, and Sargant.

Superlative tools for the study of religion through direct observation and experiment have been provided lately through the psychedelic drugs. An example is Pahnke's Good Friday experiment with psilocybin, which is a model of scientific rigor in the study of mysticism, otherwise so difficult to define and investigate.

REFERENCES

Allport, G.: The individual and his religion. New York, Macmillan, 1950.
Clark, W. H.: Chemical ecstasy: Psychedelic drugs and religion. New York, Sheed & Ward, 1969.
Clark, W. H.: The psychology of religion. New York, Macmillan, 1958.
Coe, G. A.: The psychology of religion. Chicago, University of Chicago Press, 1916.
Godin, A., S.J. (Ed.) From religious experience to a religious attitude. Chicago, Loyola University Press, 1965.
Hedgepeth, W. and Stock, D.: The Alternative, New York, Macmillan, 1970.
Houriet, R.: Getting back together. New York, McCann & Geoghegan, 1971.
Huxley, A.: The doors of perception, New York, Harper, 1963.
James, W.: The varieties of religious experience. New York, New American Library, 1958.
Johnson, P. E.: Psychology of religion. New York, Abingdon Press, 1959.
Kluckholn, Florence: The participant observer technique in small communities. American Journal of Sociology, 1940, 46, 331-343.
Laski, M: Ecstasy. Bloomington, Indiana, Indiana University Press, 1962.
Malony, H. N., Flakoll, D. A. and Warren, N. C.: Symposium on methodology in the psychology of religion. A symposium at the annual meeting of the Society for the Scientific Study of Religion, New York, October, 1970.
Metzner, R. (Ed.): The ecstatic adventure. New York, Macmillan, 1968.
Otto, R.: The idea of the holy. New York, Oxford University Press, 1958.
Pahnke, W. N.: Drugs and mysticism: An analysis of the relationship between mystical consciousness and psychedelic drugs. Harvard University Ph.D. dissertation, 1964.
Pratt, J. B.: The religious consciousness. New York, Macmillan, 1920.
Pruyser, P. W.: A dynamic psychology of religion. New York, Harper & Row, 1968.
Sargant, W.: The battle for the mind. Baltimore, Penguin Books, 1961.
Stace, W. T.: Mysticism and philosophy. Philadelphia, Lippincott, 1960.
Starbuck, E. D.: The psychology of religion. New York, Scribner, 1903.
Stark, R.: A taxonomy of religious experience. Journal for the Scientific Study of Religion, 1965, 5, (1), 97-116.
Underhill, Evelyn: Mysticism. New York, The Noonday Press, 1930.

... our normal waking consciousness, rational consciousness, as we call it, is but one special type of consciousness, whilst all about it, parted from it by the filmiest of screens, there lie potential forms of consciousness entirely different. We may go through life without suspecting their existence; but apply the requisite stimulus, and at a touch they are there in all their completeness ...

—William James

Chapter 2

THE PHENOMENA OF RELIGIOUS EXPERIENCE

WALTER HOUSTON CLARK

IN my first lecture, I said something about the place of religious experience in the history of religion and the methods by which it has been studied by varying scholars in the past and the present. But I suppose that what I would chiefly have you remember from the lecture is my emphasis on the importance of the nonrational in religion, not because I wish to exclude the rational, but because of its central importance to any lively and effective expression of religion. I marked the tendencies of the contemporary religious church to neglect religious experience and of scholars to derogate it. In this lecture, I will discuss some of the forms that religious experience takes.

THE PROBLEM OF REDUCTIONISM

Before I start on my task, I want to deal with a persistent problem that so often troubles the psychologist of religion. This is the temptation to reduce religion to one or more of its more humble origins or principles. An absurd example from another field would be to reason that since Shakespeare could not have written his plays without eating, *Hamlet* is nothing more than meat, vegetables, and English ale in another form. Thus equally absurd is the position of the Czechoslovakian government. I asked a Czech who was doing research with LSD whether the authorities there were not troubled by the fact that often subjects under LSD report profound religious experience, including what might appear to be, for a doctrinaire Communist atheist, an embarrassing experience, namely the encounter with God. "Oh no," he replied, "they simply instruct us to explain that this shows that religion is nothing but chemistry."

Such fallacies are relatively easy for us to see. Somewhat more subtle is Freud's claim that religion is nothing but the search for the father image or a regression to the state of early childhood with fantasies of wish fulfillment and magical thinking. Others have claimed that religion, variously, is simply a collection of moral rules, derives from conflict, expresses the need for protection or love, comes from an association between people, or represents the quest for life's meaning. All of these are partly true, but to overemphasize any or other sources of the religious life is to be guilty of reductionism. For religion is as broad as all of life and includes it all, even chemistry. The besetting sin of every psychologist of religion is to ride his own particular hobby too hard and so risk the charge of being a reductionist.

But the temptation of the scholar, for whom reason is a password, is to overdo the intellectual in proving that his mind is in good working order. His desire is to reduce his studies to concepts and to arrange the latter in neatly ordered categories. His problem is to retain his nonrational sense of wonder at the same time that he keeps his reason and his sense of proportion, in order to pursue his scholarly way and so produce perception and understanding for others. Only in this case will he understand that there is no theology nor dogma, no matter how distinguished or precisely stated, that alone can sustain the strange workings of faith and the religious quest. To put the matter in Christian terms, neither the Father nor the Son nor the Holy Spirit can do their work confined in an intellectual formula. One cannot pursue religion in cold blood.

WHAT IS RELIGIOUS ECSTASY?

The nonrational factor in religion is closely associated with ecstasy, at least in its more intense forms. Literally the root meaning of "ecstasy" is "a standing out of oneself" or "being beside oneself." It is a state in which the individual participates in a kind of consciousness wholly different from his normal consciousness in which he achieves perceptions so new to him that we often say, "He has transcended himself." These perceptions are usually attended with strong emotions, so that often these states are thought of as characteristically emotional in nature. However, though there doubtless is considerable interaction between the perception and the emotion, I prefer to define religious ecstasy as primarily a state of increased perceptiveness. To see it as merely emotional is to downgrade and distort its significance and to risk the reductionism about which I have been speaking.

Doubtless there is the danger of cultivating it for the pleasure and excitement that the ecstatic state produces. Under these conditions it will become shallow and unproductive and so the source of the strictures so often lavished on this type of religion by disapproving intellectuals. But individuals differ not only in the depth and perceptive quality of their ecstasies but in the use they make of their perceptions. Examined critically after they have come back to themselves — for an ecstasy observed too closely by the experiencer during the process is apt to lose its power — these perceptions will become fruitful only after they have been approved and in some manner acted on. The ecstasy of no two people is exactly the same, but ecstasy in some form has characterized most religious leaders.

In the first lecture I mentioned several of the Judeo-Chrisitan ecstatics. There I referred to their ecstasies as "religious experience," a more common term for the religious type of ecstasy. Moses perceived the presence of God when he stood in ecstasy before the burning bush, while Isaiah accepted his religious mission received in an ecstatic vision described in the 6th chapter of his prophecy. Francis of Assisi, Ignatius of Loyola, and Teresa of Avila were among the many Christian ecstatics canonized as Saints. Socrates was subject to ecstatic states, and Plato made it clear in the Allegory of the Cave in the Seventh Book of *The Republic* that he considered such states to bestow enlightenment essential for the guardians of an ideal political entity. Eastern religions abound with ecstatics, of which Gautama the Buddha, Lao-tze, and Sri Ramakrishna are only a few of the best known.

Certain rather generalized conditions are associated with and express ecstasy. Spontaneous song is one of these states while the dance is another. In one Biblical incident (II Samuel 6:14) King David "danced before the Lord with all his might." In *Battle for the Mind* (1961) the English psychiatrist William Sargant points out that primitive, exhausting religious dances often bring about religious ecstasy in such a way as to render participants more open to religious perceptions.

Another form of ecstasy expresses itself in strange utterances known as "speaking in tongues" or "glossolalia." This was the state in which the early Christian disciples found themselves on the day of Pentecost after the Resurrection and Ascension of Jesus when words spoken in several tongues seemed to be understood as one (Acts 2:1-13). There have been apparent duplications of this phenomena both in other religions and in contemporary Christianity not only in the Pentecostal sects but even in the mainline Christian churches such as the Episcopalian and Presbyterian, where it is generally disapproved by the majority of sober churchgoers. These occurrences are often reported to be followed by certain gifts in more effective attitudes and living, as I will describe later.

Here, I will discuss in greater detail the ecstatic states of conversion and mysticism, both exceedingly important in the history and development of the Christian faith. However, there is some artificiality involved in categorizing ecstatic states, for they tend to overlap one another and cannot be strictly separated.

CONVERSION

Conversion may be divided into two general varieties. First is the change of attitude toward a faith orientation from one of rejection to that of acceptance, or *vice versa*. The second is the change from a state of general religious unbelief and disintegration to one of positive integration and effectiveness of life along the lines of whatever faith commitment one has already accepted. While each of these changes may be gradual and slow, the more dramatic, and possibly more effective, are those that come suddenly and are accompanied by strong emotional tone. One may see them as two different modes of religious growth, the one slow and the other more rapid. But the term is more often used when the sudden change is meant. In general I will be using the word in this sense.

The prototype of this process, for Christians, is the experience of Saul of Tarsus on the Damascus Road, when he saw a blinding light and heard the voice of Jesus speaking to him (Acts 9:1-31). In latter days this story has led to an emphasis on conversion, particularly among evangelical Protestants, as was mentioned in the first lecture, such as the Wesleyan revival in England and nineteenth century revivalism in America. A cogent force in the twentieth century, worldwide in its scope, and nondenominational in its emphasis, has been the movement led by the late Frank Buchman known originally as Buchmanism but, since the 1920's as the Oxford Group and then Moral Rearmament. Now perhaps its chief expression is seen in "Up With People," a movement separated from though allied with Moral Rearmament which carries its message globally chiefly through young people who attract audiences in singing performances.

The movement had its beginning in the conversion experience of its founder. 1905 found Frank Buchman in a small village in England where he had gone after a dispute with the trustees of a charitable venture in Philadelphia nursing great ill will toward them. At a church service he had a vision of the suffering Christ. With the vision there came a sudden conviction of his estrangement. Like John Wesley, whose conversion was signaled when his "heart was strangely warmed," Buchman's was accompanied by a "vibrant feeling up and down the spine, as if a strong current of life were suddenly poured into me." At the same time he surrendered his life to Christ and shortly afterward wrote letters to the trustees apologizing to them (cf. Clark, 1951, p. 39).

The ecstatic elements in Buchman's conversion are sufficiently clear. His subsequent career demonstrated the strong intuitive characteristics often associated with ecstatics. The Buchman movement became in its day probably the most effective religious movement of the times. Buchman was not without his weaknesses and peculiarities, but William James was thinking about his type of temperament when he suggested that it was just this kind of person who might be expected to be most sensitive to religious inspiration (1958, p. 37). He warns us against the fallacy of idolizing the completely normal person and extolling as the aim for all persons the standard of invincible mental health. The saints and prophets of the ages have often demonstrated something less than its perfection.

The sudden conversion experience, though in many details variable, tends to follow certain well-defined stages, at least in Christianity with its emphasis on sin. There is the stage of conflict and discomfort due to a vague feeling of insufficiency and an awareness of how far one's life falls below his ideals. This stage may be characterized by a radical condition of disorganization symptomatic of dangerous mental illness. Augustine tells how for many years he vacillated between the claims of Christianity and the pleasures of the pagan life to which he had accustomed himself.

The next stage is the crisis itself, perhaps ushered in by a confession of sin or by some other stimulus leading to a surrender to God's will with a consequent relaxation of tension that brings with it great relief. In Augustine's case the stimulus was an apparent auditory hallucination that sent him to the Bible and a chance turning to a passage that sealed his decision to turn Christian, after which all his lesser decisions seemed to fall easily into place.

This latter phase in Augustine's case illustrates the third phase of conversion following the climactic point. This leaves the convert with a sense of peace, harmony, and a sense of inner integration that brings with it a sense of freedom and power. Of course this latter creative stage, so delightful to the convert, does not last unless it is rigorously followed up, which entails an active self-discipline and a critical conscience if the convert is to avoid backsliding and continued mental distress (cf. Clark, 1958, Chapt. 9).

Following Starbuck, James distinguishes between what he calls the *volitional* and *self-surrender* types of conversion (1958, p. 169). Volitional conversion is a more gradual type which involves much more of the element of the conscious will and other rational processes. This comes much closer to what we see as a process of natural growth and therefore it is much more popular with students of religious education, who very naturally desire something to study and perhaps to control. Such a process is much freer of the kinds of surprises and crises that can throw the well-oiled gears of ecclesiastical machinery out of alignment.

It is not that the crisis type of conversion cannot be controlled also. It is too much of this catering to safety that has brought the practice of conversion to the surface of consciousness and so robbed it of its spontaneity and its power. But if crisis conversion has certain superiorities over the more gradual type – and I think it has – it is that it derives its power from deeper levels of the human psyche, where more primitive impulses have their being. Part of the ability of the awareness of the convert to break through to this level comes from the suddenness with which it occurs, just as the burning of a stick of dynamite occurs with suddenness when it is confined. Thus the resulting explosion does work that could not be accomplished if applied with a more "genteel" type of forcefulness, so to speak. In my *Psychology of Religion* (1958) I have called this phenomenon *conversion shock*.

MYSTICISM

I now turn to what is probably the most captivating and transforming experience of which human nature is capable. I am referring to mystical experience. We cannot precisely separate mysticism from conversion, for mysticism tends to be equally sudden. And it reaches down to an even deeper layer of the soul. Furthermore, most mystical experiences mark a conversion involving perceptions that lead to a radical change of values. As I have continued my studies in the psychology of religion through the years, more and more I have shifted my earlier interest and belief in conversion to a more recent concern with mysticism because I have come to realize its richer possibilities. It represents a riper and more penetrating form of spiritual awakening and growth.

I have no illusions about there being anything very original in my stand. William James gave his opinion that mysticism is the "root and center" of personal religion (1958, p. 292). Evelyn Underhill, a mystic herself, has written several scholarly volumes on the subject, while Princeton's late professor of Philosophy, W. T. Stace, has been only the most distinguished recent American scholar to treat the subject systematically with an enlightening and thoroughly scholarly rigor.

There has always been a strong and healthy tradition of mysticism within Christianity, stemming originally from neo-Platonism and particularly marked in the Medieval church. It is probably the mystical element which, more than any other single feature, explains the amazing and perennial vigor of Catholic Christianity. But it has always had to contend with the even stronger tradition of rationalism, in all branches of Christianity, to which I have already referred in my first lecture. This has led to its neglect, which helps to explain the thinness, blandness, and harmlessness of much that passes for Christianity in many of our churches.

There is a sense in which, as we approach these areas of conversion and mysticism, the student on such sacred ground may be felt to be an intruder. For those who experience religious ecstasy are not in the slightest degree interested in an analysis of the process they are undergoing. If they were it would only be as an interference and a hindrance. The initiative does not seem to come from within themselves but from God, or some source far beyond themselves. Like Paul confronted by Jesus on the Damascus road, or Francis Thompson, as he so beautifully described his pilgrimage in "The Hound of Heaven" (Manly 1926), the convert may feel relentlessly though lovingly pursued by an awesome power greater than himself. To study such experiences may appear almost blasphemous. To attempt to analyze them with rational tools may seem like trying to study the beauty of a snowflake armed with a blowtorch and iron tongs. We may be skirting perilously the borders of reductionism, about which I have already warned you.

However, if the reason and rationality is to have any place in directing the religious life, we must have knowledge to help guide us. If I thought it blasphemous to study religious experience I would not be talking about the subject. My intent is to approach my subject with as much knowledge and intelligence as I can muster at the same time that I must acknowledge that the roots of these experiences reach far beyond my sight in the infinite depths and recesses of the holy. In dealing with mysticism I will simply try to describe the experience so that it can be recognized, even though never completely understood, within yourselves or in other people, and then say something of conditions that favor its appearance.

MYSTICISM: ITS PHENOMENA

One of the characteristics of mysticism, universally recognized, is the difficulty one has in describing it. For this reason most people look on it as foggy, dubious, and even esoteric. This presents any scholar who wishes to describe it with a dilemma. He is asked to describe the indescribable, to utter the unutterable. Great Eastern mystics have been known to recommend total silence on the subject. But Western scholars have nevertheless attacked the subject in characteristic Western fashion. Probably the most successful and incisive of these has been W. T. Stace in his *Mysticism and Philosophy* (1960). Much of my description is dependent on him.

To prepare for his analysis, Stace studied the literature of mysticism in all ages and all faiths. From this he abstracted seven characteristics which appeared over and over again in widely scattered and largely unrelated sources. These seven characteristics he called "the universal core" of mysticism. They appeared in accounts given by Christians, Hasidic Jews, Mohammedan Sufis, Hindus, Buddhists, and Taoists. It would seem that the capacity for mysticism is a natural gift of God, possessed probably by all men though, as with other gifts, not in equal abundance in all.

The first and probably the most essential of Stace's characteristics is the experience of unity, in which all sense impressions and specific awareness of the sensible world drops away and the mystic feels himself to have encountered what may be variously described as "the Void," "the boundless Sea," "the white light," or simply "Infinity." In a well-known couplet the English mystic Henry Vaughan wrote:

I saw Eternity the other night
Like a great Ring of pure and endless light

The effect of such experiences is to give the mystic a feeling of his identity with all things. Consequently he knows that every man is his brother; he experiences directly the feelings that he and his enemy are one and so becomes capable of loving him. It is out of such knowledge that the often noted compassion of the mystic springs. It is significant that it was a mystic who wrote the lines, "Never send to enquire for whom the bell tolls; it tolls for thee."

Derived from the experience of unity comes the next characteristic, the experience of timelessness and spacelessness. Our sense of time comes from the perception of a series of images or events, while space derives from a sense of self set amongst the perception of objects and images surrounding one. Consequently the sense of time and space are closely intertwined. When the conception of these images melt into an undifferentiated oneness, it follows that any perceptions dependent on them will fall away also. It is in such a way that not the reasoned concept of time and space but the immediate experience of them will melt away. It was after a mystical event that solved his problems and taught him compassion for his neighbor that Thomas Carlyle, in his fine spiritual autobiography *Sartor Resartus* declared:

On the roaring billows of Time, thou art not engulfed, but borne aloft into the azure of Eternity. Love not pleasure; love God (1896, 174-175).

To the nonmystic this last quotation may seem a dark saying, but it leads us to Stace's third characteristic. It is the sense of having been in touch with some sort of objectivity or ultimate reality. In Christianity the name for this reality is God, and the Christian mystics have nearly always identified this reality as the Father, or one of the other members of the Trinity, or the Trinity itself, as with Saint Teresa of Avila on one occasion. It is such a reality that gives meaning to life and along with this a fortitude, strength, and courage that to those standing by are sources of amazement. Such steadfastness on the part of Stephen helped to convert Paul; the spectacle of Christian martyrs meeting death in the forum with singing were seeds of the early Church; while the sight of heretics being burned alive to the glory of God by the Inquisition in later days touched the minds of many and helped bring about the Reformation.

The effects of these encounters with unity and reality are also such as to leave the mystic with feelings of blessedness, joy, and peace — the fourth characteristic. "The peace of God which passes all understanding" is a phrase all of us have heard at the end of a religious service and have been impressed with its beauty, though few of us have ever ascribed it to a mystic. Also this characteristic will help us better to understand the many references to joy in the Bible, a characteristic of religion that many of our churches seem to have forgotten.

Closely associated with all of the foregoing characteristics is Stace's fifth category of the feeling of holiness, the sacred, or the divine. Otto would round out this feeling with allusions to the terror and awe often associated with the presence of the divine, as when the Lord approached Abram, who felt himself overcome by "an horror of great darkness" (Genesis 15:12), or the statement of the writer of Hebrews to the effect that "it is a fearful thing to fall into the hands of the living God" (Hebrews 10:31). More than any of the other categories this is the most specifically religious.

A further characteristic is the claim by the mystics that their experiences are unutterable or ineffable. They have often likened their dilemma to that of one trying to describe the experience of sight to a race born blind. The stuttering attempts of the sighted to convince his hearers that there really does exist a sense transcending those that they have would only mark him as peculiar and queer, a laughing stock to the uncomprehending ones. He would either give up the attempt and remain silent, or with a frustrated eloquence vainly reiterate the perceptions so wonderfully vouchsafed to him whose eyes had been illumined. The latter is the lot of many mystics who cannot help believing that God wishes to illumine with his Presence all those to whom He has granted human life.

The fact that there is no literal way adequately to convey to a nonmystic the essence of the mystical consciousness requires that the mystic use riddles, figures of speech, and other out-of-the-way means to suggest his meaning. Thus the mystics become the poets and artists of the religious life. To convey the beauty of the sunset to him who has been born blind, one might liken it to the effect of a symphony. The imaginative blindman would get the point even though he could never experience directly the sight of the sunset itself. Thus the value of the simile.

The most common figure of speech or riddle through which the mystics attempt to resolve their frustration is paradox – and this is the last of Stace's seven characteristics of mysticism. Logically inconsistent, paradox, nevertheless, often conveys more perceptively and movingly than everyday speech the essence of the experience toward which it points. Thus if the mystic refers to his perception as "the Void," he may also describe it as a "full void." In the literature of mysticism we find very common such expressions as "dazzling darkness," "teeming desert," "wayless path," or "dark silence."

It will be instructive here to contrast the method of the theologian and that of the mystic to convey the meaning of the word "God." The theologian might present a list of adjectives, such as "omnipotent, omniscient, just, merciful, loving, etc." But listen to a mystic's attempt to convey his immediate perception of God. The words are those of Jan Van Ruysbroeck, a Medieval Dutch brother:

> The abysmal waylessness of God is so dark and so unconditioned that it swallows up within itself every Divine way and activity, and all the attributes of the persons within the essential unity . . . .This is the dark silence in which all lovers lose themselves. But if we would prepare ourselves for it . . . we should strip ourselves of all but our very bodies, and we should flee forth into the wild sea, whence no created thing can draw us back again (cf Stace, 1960, p. 97).

Both the method of the theologian and the mystic have their own value, but any of you who to any degree found yourselves moved by the poetic beauty of the Ruysbroeck passage can know that this testifies to the mystic sleeping deeply within yourselves and that in essence you too are mystics.

I have not the time to review the analyses of mysticism listed by two other keen students of the mystical life, namely William James and Evelyn Underhill, though I will mention one or two of their points in passing. James refers to the transiency of the mystical state. Though Gautama averred that an achievement of perpetual Nirvana, the Buddhist name for the mystical conscious- ness, was possible, and certain Eastern mystics have claimed they have attained it, it seems extremely unlikely that a constant high level of spiritual bliss could be attained in this life. Though the essence of the state may be a perception, nevertheless the resulting emotion attendant on the attainment of a state of consciousness so different, delightful, and new could hardly be expected to last indefinitely without fluctuation. Furthermore the demands of everyday life, at the very least of clothing and housing and feeding oneself would be apt to interrupt the state of vision. Practically speaking, I think we can expect these states normally not to exceed more than two hours at most, while a half hour or less would seem more usual. However, the aura of the experience may last for many days, and its influence for a lifetime.

On another point James and Underhill are at odds. James mentions passivity as a characteristic of the mystical state while Underhill marks the fact that "true mysticism is active and practical" (1955, p. 81 ff.). Doubtless the difference can be resolved if we separate the state of mind during ecstasy, which must be totally accepting and, as Underhill states herself, "an act of surrender," from the attitude afterward. Many mystics, like Teresa of Avila, have lived confused and ineffective lives before their visions, while afterward their lives have become marvels of practical activity. It is true that there is the danger of what the Catholic Church has branded "quietism," when the attainment of ecstasy may become a form of self-indulgence with few construc- tive results. But more often the state will mark a person's coming to himself and achieving what Erik Erikson might call his essential "identity."

MYSTICISM: ITS TRIGGERS

To ask the question "What causes mysticism?" would involve us in theological and metaphysical issues far beyond my scope as a psychologist. The religious mystic sees the cause of his moving experience as God, and nothing that the psychologist will say can controvert this perception and commitment of faith. I will simply point out conditions which seem to favor the mystical state. Perhaps we can best talk of these conditions as "triggers" which set off a chain of internal events physiological and neurological in character to heighten perceptivity and so make ready sensitivity to respond to these conditions. What then are some of these triggers?

But before we turn to the subject of triggers let me call your attention to what Stace calls "The Principle of Causal Indifference" (1960, pp. 29-31). Stace refers to what I have called "triggers" as "causes" of mystical experience. We are both referring to what I think we would both agree are favoring circumstances. There is a tendency for some people to hold that if the trigger is trivial, artificial, or contrived, then the resulting experience cannot be "genuine," whatever that may mean. Stace's principle states that no matter what the trigger, if the phenomena fits the definition of mysticism it is just as "genuine" as any other mystical experience. My experience in the use of drugs to evoke religious experience causes me to agree.

One of the best discussions of triggers for mystical experience is to be found in Marghanita Laski's *Ecstasy* (1962, pp. 176-277). Not all of the cases of ecstasy reviewed in her excellent study are religious, but many are, and her general comments refer to both types. Her discussion will illustrate most of my following generalizations. A further feature of the Laski study is that she points out what she calls "anti-triggers," the sights and symbols of mundane, crass, and practical living that tend to "turn off" ecstasy.

Probably one thing that prepares a person for a mystical experience is to know that there is such a thing. The purpose of much religious liturgy is to suggest it, from the rich Catholic Mass to the simple Quaker silence. In this way the reading of scripture can be a general trigger as well as spiritual biography and even the hearing of a lecture such as this, as I hope it may in many of you. I have known of several people who have reported that ecstasy was preceded by the reading of the sympathetic pages of William James' *Varieties of Religious Experience* (1958). It is also a favorable condition for a potential mystic to know that mysticism is approved of. Otherwise these holy impulses will be mistaken for oddity or even signs of oncoming mental illness. In such cases they will be repressed and spiritual growth hindered.

Typical triggers are found in abundance in the world of nature, as mystical poets so often remind us. William Blake wrote:

> To see the world in a grain of sand
>> And a heaven in a wild flower
> To hold Infinity in the palm of your hand
>> Eternity in an hour (Yeats, no dat, p. 90).

Clouds, sky, violent storms, green grass, and tender flowers may initiate impulses or, as Shakespeare put it,

> . . . antres vast and deserts idle
> Rough quaries, rocks, and hills whose heads touch heaven (1879, p. 51).

A trigger related to some of the foregoing is sensory deprivation. Agnostic psychologists who have confined subjects in dark, silent rooms to see what would happen have been surprised, not to say even frightened, when some have reported religious visions and experiences. This throws light on the preference of some ecstatics for the "antres vast" (dark caves), silence, or other monotonous surroundings like the desert, the wilderness, or the vast wastes of the sea. Moses met Jehovah in the burning bush on the wild slopes of Horeb, while St. Anthony came to his spiritual majority in his encounter with visions in the depths of a cave. This is one of the purposes of the Gregorian chant or plainsong, otherwise a stumbling block to the literal-minded.

Another is the attitude of complete surrender, the willingness to accept whatever may come in utter passivity and open-mindedness. "Here am I," said Isaiah following his vision, "Send me" (Isaiah 6:8). Often the mystical state is completely unintended and accompanies a period of exhaustion or enforced relaxation following an illness, as with St. Francis and St. Ignatius of Loyola. This may help to explain why mystical experience sometimes follows childbirth or other trauma. Exhaustion is sometimes brought on deliberately for religious purposes not just in previous times or in primitive religious ceremonies but contemporaneously among the Penitente sects in the southwest and Mexico, the snake-handling sects of the southern back-country, or the marathon worship in some Pentecostal services (cf. Sargant, 1961,

Chapters 5-8). Exhaustion makes possible complete relaxation and willingness to accept whatever experience comes without fighting it or trying to control it. Thus perfect surrender might be called one of God's hand maidens.

A final trigger is biochemical change within the body. Doubtless some people probably are more susceptible to mysticism due to their physiological makeup, just as others are conditioned by their makeup to be poets or musicians. Others deliberately manipulate biochemical changes by fasting or the use of a special diet, like the macrobiotic. Still others, more directly, either inject or ingest certain drugs, the most popular currently being the psychedelics. At this point Stace's Principle of Causal Indifference is helpful to us in calming the stormy sea of controversy surrounding this troublesome area. Dr. Walter N. Pahnke, in a Harvard experiment carried out on Good Friday with Christian theological students as subjects, mentioned in my first lecture, clearly showed that psilocybin greatly enhanced the phenomena of mysticism in a favorable environment. I have confirmed this in my own experiments (cf. Clark, 1969, p. 77). Breathing exercises, chanting, incense, in part are means of biochemical intervention, whether realized or not, while inadevertent changes in diet, fasting, or other unconscious production of bodily change may release the mystical. However, the conscious aiming at religious experience seems always to make it more likely though not inevitable.

The foregoing discussion of the triggers of mystical experience, of course, must be considered as the merest of introductions to what is a wide, complicated, fascinating and important field both for the theoretical and practical understanding of the religious life.

MYSTICISM: ITS PLACE IN PERSONALITY

In the foregoing description of mysticism, I must reiterate, I have been describing the common psychological core of mysticism. It is probable that, could the Buddha and Van Ruysbroek have met, they would have found a common fellowship enabling them to communicate with one another better than with many of their nonmystical associates in their own tradition. They would speak a common language, for they soon would learn that what one called "Nirvana" and the other "union with Christ" are psychologically identical, or at least very similar, experiences. But in another respect they would be far apart, for each would interpret his experience in terms of his own faith and his own culture. Here their language would be different and would separate the *interpretation* of the mystical state from its psychological or "universal" core, as Stace indicates.

This conclusion suggests that, since the fundamental experience is deeper than its interpretation, we should ignore the latter and live together on the basis of the equality of all faiths. In a sense, mysticism might well become acknowledged as a common religious experience and could become a powerful influence for bringing together separate faiths and warring nations. Indeed it is probably the only force that has any chance of allaying the dangerous antagonism of our times. However, not all interpretations of religious experience are identical, nor are they identical in value. Furthermore religious traditions are apt to have certain worth to those who have been brought up in them and understand them. But mutual respect for and participation in mystical states may open doors to understandings in such a way as to promote a tolerance, and open-mindedness that will result in dialogue and contacts of a healing nature.

But before I close this lecture I would like to say a word about the relation of religious experience to the unconscious, which may help to give us a background for remarks in my last lecture. The comments I am about to make are partly speculative but are based on research done in Czechoslovakia at the Psychiatric Research Institute in Prague by Dr. Stanislav Grof and colleagues (cf. Clark, 1969, pp. 109-113).

In this research psychotics and severe neurotics were given LSD every week or more for up to thirty administrations. After from twelve to sixteen administrations to the typical patient, symptoms had rather steadily improved. Freudian symbolism indicated the exploration of the personal unconscious with references to Oedipal problems and other stages of the typical Freudian growth pattern. Then symptoms suddenly worsened when Rankian symbolism began to appear. Here there were traces of actual memories of the experience of birth and the arousal of frightening feelings of the facing of death. But this was followed, usually rather suddenly, by an experience of rebirth and of freedom with a likeness to many classical experiences of creative psychological rebirth such as "death and transfiguration" or Jesus' statement that to see salvation one must be "born again" (John 3:3-11).

Usually this period was rather brief, but it was followed by a stage in which symbolism related by the patients turned Jungian in nature. You will recall that Jung made statements to the effect that he had never treated a patient over the age of thirty-five when the problem did not turn out to be religious in nature. It was during this stage that Grof's patients reported symbolism of an archetypal and mystical nature. Also it was during this stage that the patients not only achieved normality but usually went on to a positively creative one. If they came back to the Institute for further treatment, as a few of them did, it was for different problems from those that had driven them into treatment in the first place. The development of normal subjects was similar but more rapid.

The significance of this research for our purposes is that it suggests that transcendental religious experiences come from a layer of the personality far deeper than that usually recognized as the unconscious. Perhaps a Freudian psychoanalysis is simply a preliminary phase which, if limited by Freud's otherwise brilliant theories and practice, would fall far short of those transformations that can only be effected when the religious dimension, as suggested by Rankian and more especially Jung, is involved (see Fig. 1).

Perhaps also these speculations will help us to understand why intellectual, rational, and discursive thinking is so weak in enabling man to change his ways. He remains on the surface of life and is confined to mending the roof of the structure. This often has to be done, but when the problem is with the foundations it is only when the foundations are exposed that truly transforming changes can be expected. For these reasons we can begin to understand more clearly those amazing life changes that so often only religious experience can effect. To explore these will be the task of the final lecture.

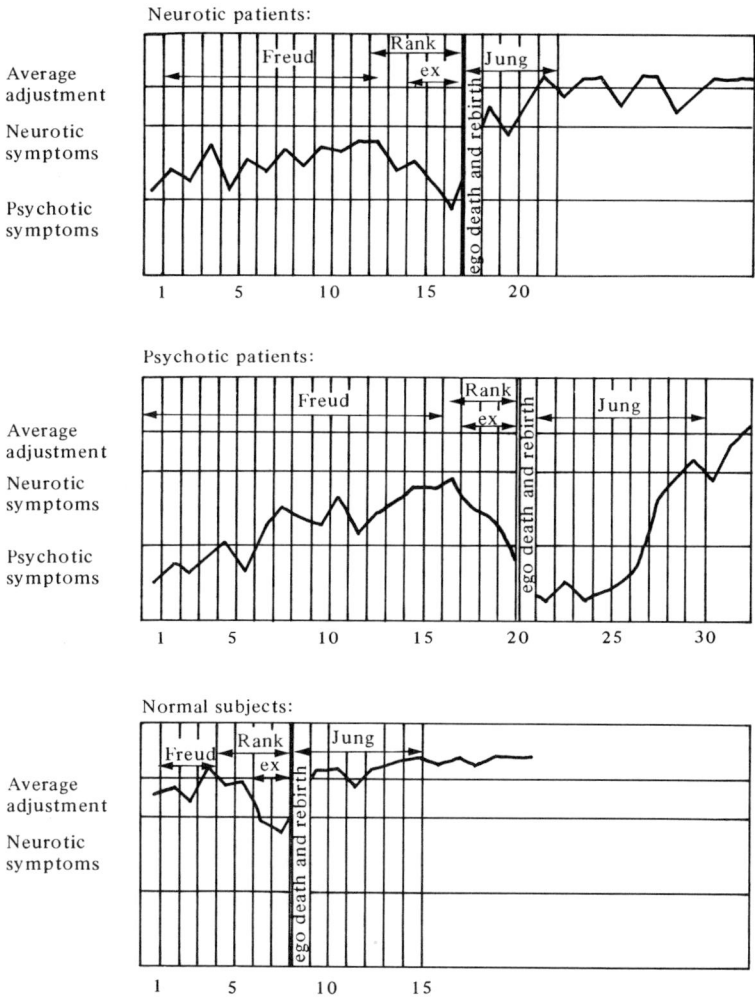

Figure 1. Representing clinical condition of three typical subjects in free intervals between sessions in successful psycholytic treatment with LSD-25.

Vertical Axis: clinical condition.

Horizontal Axis: number of LSD sessions.

Ex: existential experience.

(Figure used with the permission of Dr. Stanislav Grof and taken from his forthcoming book *The Theory and Practice of LSD Therapy* soon to be published by the University of Pennsylvania Press.)

SUMMARY

The psychologist of religion must beware of the fallacy of thinking he can reduce religious experience to the factors he can uncover and understand and therefore of missing its ultimate mystery. This lecture has concentrated on various forms of religious ecstasy, sometimes expressed in song, dance, or strange forms of utterance like glossalia. A better known form of ecstasy is sudden conversion, when a person's values may dramatically change or conflicting elements in his personality suddenly come together, as with John Wesley when his "heart was strangely warmed." Since ecstasy brings one in touch with unconscious powers, such conversions are frequently more effective and durable than the slower type involving gradual growth. But these conversions always need the support of discipline and development of slower growth if the convert is to avoid backsliding.

But the deepest religious force of all is provided by mystical ecstasy, the most transforming and captivating experience of which human nature is capable. Stace identifies the persistent psychological characteristics reported by mystics of all faiths and ages as the sense of universal unity: timelessness and spacelessness; the sense of an ultimate objective reality; blessedness, joy, and peace; the feeling of being in touch with the holy; ineffability; and the tendency to use paradox. James speaks of the transiency of the experience, while Underhill states that the true mystic leads an active rather than a passive life. The difficulty in describing their experiences forces the mystics to become the poets and the artists of the religious life. Some triggers of mysticism include informative reading, instruction, and appropriate liturgy; scenes of natural beauty or majesty; sensory monotony or deprivation; the "surrender" that accompanies weakness or exhaustion; and biochemical intervention such as can be provided through fasting, special breathing exercises, and drugs. Stace's Principle of Causal indifference states that it is not the trigger but the phenomenology of the experience that determines whether or not an experience is truly mystical. But while these characteristics of mysticism are universal, they should be distinguished from their interpretation, which differs from faith to faith.

Important research relative to the structure of the human unconscious has been done by Grof in Czechoslovakia with LSD-25. This disclosed Freudian, Rankian, and Jungian elements in succeeding layers of depth. Particularly the Rankian, with its psychological death and rebirth, and the Jungian levels of archetypal depth, suggested sources of ecstatic power.

REFERENCES

Augustinus, Aurelius: The confessions, trans. by J. G. Pilkington. New York, Boni and Liveright, 1927.

Carlyle, T.: Sartor resartus. Boston, Ginn and Company, 1896.

Clark, W. H.: The Oxford Group. New York, Bookman Associates, 1951.

Clark, W. H.: The psychology of religion. New York, Macmillan, 1958.

Clark, W. H.: Chemical ecstasy. Psychedelic drugs and religion, New York, Sheed and Ward, 1969.

James, W.: The varieties of religious experience. New York, New American Library, 1958.

Laski, M.: Ecstasy. Bloomington, Indiana, Indiana University Press, 1962.

Manly, J. M. (Ed): English prose and poetry, Revised Edition: Boston, Ginn, 1926.

Sargant, W.: The battle for the mind. Baltimore, Penguin Books, 1961.

Shakespeare, W.: Othello. New York, Harper, 1879.

Stace, W. T.: Mysticism and philosophy. Philadelphia, Lippincott, 1960.

Underhill, E.: Mysticism, New York, The Noonday Press, 1955.

Yeats, W. B. (Ed): Poems of William Blake. New York, The Modern Library, no date.

Earth might be fair and all men glad and wise.
Age after age their tragic empires rise,
Built while they dream, and in that dreaming weep;
Would man but wake from out his haunted sleep,
Earth might be fair and all men glad and wise.

— Clifford Bax

Chapter 3

THE INFLUENCE OF
RELIGIOUS EXPERIENCE

WALTER HOUSTON CLARK

IN the preceding lectures, I reviewed the place and function of religious experience and its common phenomena. I will now talk about the *effects* of religious experience. Those who have never participated in religious ecstasy or, if they have, have never followed it up through discipline or a testing of its insights, often come to the easy conclusion that it is a religious form of self-indulgence, an escape into a narrow subjectivism, or a kind of religious form of exhibitionism. Without denying that many examples can be found to support such dismal appraisals, I am going to remain content to warn you that if it be true that all that glitters is not gold, so is it true that not all that sounds pious or looks pious is necessarily the real thing. Here it should not be necessary to do more than remind you of the parable of the sower (Matt. 13:3ff.). In what follows, I am going to confine myself to speaking of the seed that falls on good ground. I will try to demonstrate to you that religious experiences may not only bring the individual a transforming vision but may also be an entry into a new life of increased delight and effectiveness.

The test I propose in demonstrating the value, or lack of it, of religious experiences is an ancient one, namely that voiced by Jesus when he told his disciples that prophets were to be known by their fruits (Matt. 7:16). William James (1958) voiced the same pragmatic principle when he said that religious experience was not to be judged by its origins but by its results. Thus I will seek to point out wholesome developments, both for the individual and society, such as personal integration, love, joy, compassion, energy, and the capacity to widen one's sympathies and sense of responsibility, as indicators of wholesome religious experiences. In doing so, I will at places refer back to some of the religious states, movements, and ideas I have already noted in previous lectures.

Of the latter, I would like to remind you first of what I have said of the function of rational processes in the guidance and control of equally essential nonrational components; and also what I have said of the tendency of the rational to be so overemphasized in Western religion as to sap religion's energy and richness. We *rationalize* religion in the Freudian sense of giving good reasons for building defenses against doing anything not proper, conventional, and safe. We become unwilling to take chances or to allow others to make mistakes, forgetting that the only persons who never make mistakes are dead men and that every live religion has a place for passion.

The duty of reason is to calculate and direct the chances that we take so that as far as possible the dangers are faced and courage does not degenerate into foolhardiness. This means that the religious person must be willing at times to break through his carefully built defenses, those comfortable illusions that hide him from himself. In other words, he must consent to become *vulnerable* if his religion is to release his creative possibilities. This vulnerability may be acquired in various ways — through witness and confession, encounter groups, communal disciplines such as living in monasteries or communes, or celebrative activities as in Pentecostal groups. Trauma of either a physical or psychological nature may bring our hidden selves to the surface, as may also certain therapeutic techniques like psychoanalysis, while careful and thoughtful use of the psychedelic drugs have often effected dramatic release in certain individuals. These means are all either explicitly religious or may be used religiously. Their religious use all involve, at some point, the act of *surrender,* surrender to God's will, to facing death, to a specific religious commitment, to the Unknown, or it may be even surrender to a "holy terror," the *mysterium tremendum* of which Otto speaks.

All of these events may be part or even all of what some people mean when they speak of God, who appears to men in various ways and to no two quite alike. He even appears to those who do not use His name, as with certain Buddhists, and I have known fierce atheists who have worshipped Him, like the citizens of Athens, without knowing who He was. James speaks of the atheist whose friends said, "He believes in No-God, and he worships him!" But still, at some point, the religious man must acknowledge to himself and before God, by whatever name, his sinfulness, weaknesses, and essential dependency in an act of profound surrender.

But let me be more specific in pointing out some of the evidence that the psychological modes of religion described in my previous lecture have effected durable personality change. This does not always involve a change in life style. Paul was the same zealous servant of his ideals before his conversion as after it. In cases like this, it involves a change in values. But often it will involve a change in personal integration and effectiveness in living. Most often it involves both because it presents the individual with a new life that has meaning, the greatest gift of which the world is capable.

CONVERSION

I have pointed out previously the fact that conversion and mysticism are related phenomena and also that the suddenness of a religious experience often marks a deeper and more durable change in the personality than changes of slower growth. To a certain degree I have already documented this point but will simply add to that evidence and go a little more deeply into the reasons for it at this point.

In my *Chemical Ecstasy,* I start the book with the most dramatic case of conversion known to me personally, a case to which I have given well over 75 hours of careful follow-up over the years. It is the case of a lifelong, confirmed criminal, given psilocybin by Dr. Timothy Leary in a prison hospital ward. He had a vision in which he helped Christ carry his cross during the Crucifixion. Afterward, he told me, "When I looked out of the window, all my life came before my eyes, and I said, 'What a waste!' " It was his moment of surrender. Since then, he has become the co-founder of a group of convicts inside the prison to work to rehabilitate themselves and others. When he was finally released, penniless, he was offered 300 dollars a week by an underworld friend to take a job in the loan business. He turned it down. "I was tempted," he admitted to me, "but I knew what kind of business it would be, and that if I took it, I would lose the inner freedom I gained at the time of my vision!"

Freedom has not solved all of his problems, but he has made up his mind about crime. For 30 years he had constantly been in and out of jail. This time he has already been out four years, or more than four times as long as ever before. Many factors probably influenced his commitment to a God that in his hard, cynical life he had not even believed in. He had been in and out of solitary confinement. He had done much reading and even attended a prison chapel service now and then if he thought it would help his parole and hasten his return to his career of armed robbery. But for the first time in his life, he had met a man he had felt he could trust, who was trying to make it possible for him to have a religious experience. Dr. Leary taught him not to fight the experience under the drug but to accept it. This made possible the surrender, while several years of striving with his group supplied the follow-up and discipline so important in making stick any radical break with one's past life. Thus we can catch a glimpse of some of the factors at work.

Another slant on conversion, even though it is hard to generalize the theories to all cases, is found in the fascinating and suggestive volume *Battle for the Mind* by William Sargant, (1961), mentioned in the last lecture. During World War II, Sargant had noted that phobias due to tension and terrifying experiences in battle could often be reversed if the terror could be relived under hypnotic drugs in the presence of a supportive therapist. Sargant likens this to the dramatic change in temperament demonstrated by some of Pavlov's dogs under terrifying circumstances when carefully built up reflexes were suddenly wiped out. These reversals then became very resistant to subsequent change. It was as if both the animals and men under terror had reached a point of nervous exhaustion that led to a surrender and a susceptibility to change that could then be reversed again only by an equivalent trauma.

These reflections led Sargant to note that something similar was going on in surprising cases of reversal of opinions after successful procedures of brainwashing. Not all prisoners, but many of them, after prolonged periods of carefully planned torture then subjection to propaganda, could be brought to exhaustion, when they would become very suggestible. At this point, the propaganda would be again presented by a sympathetic interrogator, at which point the settled convictions of years would be swept away and the desired opinions substituted.

It was when Sargant browsed in his parson father's library that he came across an account of the Wesleyan revivals and noted that with the accounts of hell in his sermons, Wesley often brought people to such a state of nervous collapse. Following these terrifying accounts, Wesley would present the offer of salvation through the love of Jesus, which would lead to surrender and commitment to the Christian life. It was characteristic of Wesley's genius that he did not leave his converts at this point but formed them into closely knit small groups which met, often at four in the morning before the drudgery in the English factories began, to sing hymns, pray, and examine their religious condition. It was in this way, historians tell us, that the moral face of England was changed during a single generation.

Sargant goes on to give illustrations of this theory in various tribes and primitive religions. A cogent illustration is his account of the snake-handling Christian sects in back-country communities in the southern United States. In the process of demonstrating the truth of Biblical passages, leaders handle dangerous serpents during evangelical services, the result of which is that many worshippers collapse from the tension and fear. The pastor and his co-wokers then approach the semi-conscious, but at this point very suggestible, worshippers with the offer of conversion. The acceptance of

Jesus Christ at this stage, according to Sargant, often results in a commitment that endures.

Now I do not suppose that these pictures of Christian evangelism have particularly edified you. There are manifest dangers, not only in the actual deaths reported of serpent stings but in the danger of any exhausting type of evangelism with sensitive and fragile natures. Sargant himself is at pains to point out the importance of integrity on the part of church leaders using any of these methods, partly through the story of the young man — I guess you might call him an emissary of Satan — who found that pretty young women in a state of collapse due to serpent handling tended to be equally amenable to suggestions of seduction as they might have been to the call of Christ, if only he could reach them before the pastor.

At this point in our study, I do not want to assume the position of the lordly intellectual who from his eminence understands and rejects such benighted forms of Christianity. I certainly have no wish to join the snake cults, nor do I even think I would have made a good Methodist convert had I lived in John Wesley's time. Yet I cannot be sure that I have done even a fraction of the good that may have been done by the sincere and intrepid leaders of the snake cults, while it is obvious that I am far from being the servant of God manifested in John Wesley. But it is clear once again that every religion has the need for the nonrational aspects of conversion experience to be balanced by a critical rationality, whether this comes in the form of a well-organized discipline of follow-up or a theology that, at the same time that it acknowledges the place of the nonrational in religion, provides it with direction and integration.

Sargant may have overemphasized his somewhat mechanical theory of conversion, as I think he has, but he does call our attention to the importance in some cases of the wearing down of the spirit to that point where it is open and vulnerable. Maybe this was what Jesus meant when he said that those of us who wish to enter the Kingdom must become like little children. Certainly Augustine, in his years of hesitancy between the life of indulgence that he so loved and the appeal of the high adventure of commitment to Christ taught him by his mother, had reached a point of intolerable tension suddenly resolved by surrender to the words of Scripture to which he felt he had been divinely led.

In that difficult yet splendid spiritual autobiography, *Sartor Resartus,* Thomas Carlyle, tells us that, worn out by the stress of conflict and doubt he calls by the picturesque title of the "Everlasting No," he found himself in a state of comparative spiritual apathy, which he calls the "Center of Indifference." It was the awakening from this state that led him into the "Everlasting Yea" of a positive religion which showed him that higher than happiness was blessedness. "Love not pleasure; love God, wherein all contradiction is solved; wherein whoso walks and works, it is well with him" (cf. Clark, 1958, p. 198).

Another form of conversion is found in Pentecostalism, where the experience of conversion and commitment is usually called "the Baptism of the Holy Spirit" (cf. Gerlack and Hine, 1968, pp. 23-40, Hine, 1969, pp. 211-226). Commonly this is thought of as the first instance in which an individual participates in glossolalia or "speaking in tongues." To the outsider, this appears to be merely uttering strange sounds consisting of nonsense syllables, though participants claim that the capacity to speak a "sacred" language is bestowed upon them by the Holy Spirit, as with the disciples of Christ on the day of Pentecost. They relax and the sounds seem to come of their own accord, like automatic writing.

Puzzling though all of this may be to the conventional Christian, who is apt to regard such things with a jaundiced, not to say hostile, eye, many sober investigators have reported impressive personal and social benefits that seem to derive from this ecstatic behavior. It is not clear just what psychological mechanisms are involved, though it seems that the process involves giving expression to certain urges from the unconscious. In other words, it is one way in which man becomes vulnerable, departs from the straitened forms of conventional religion, and discovers a freedom to be himself which surprises and delights him as much as it alarms his friends and non-Pentecostal relatives. I have myself attended one such service of my own denomination, and though I am sorry to say I enjoyed no baptism, nevertheless I can testify to a joy, spontaneity, and friendliness unusual in other services to which I am accustomed. Snare drums, tambourines, the embrace of

Christian love from total strangers, and ecstatic utterances are just not the things usually to be expected in the Protestant Episcopal Church.

But the researches of Gerlach and Hine (1968) of the University of Minnesota, and of others, speak of conversion experiences among Pentecostals that carry over into other fields, such as better-integrated family life among the upper classes. Among the lower classes, as in certain Latin American communities, Pentecostals previously slipshod and unemployable have followed their Baptism of the Holy Spirit by becoming well-integrated members of their congregations and have been sought after by firms seeking reliable help. These researchers speak of certain social aspects of these movements that help to explain the support and follow-up so essential to an enduring conversion. As scientific researchers, however, they are not so apt to mention that sincere belief in God and the Trinity that I would assume to be important in such settings. Furthermore, contrary to what might be expected, most studies have shown that glossolaliacs tend not to be the freaks and problem members of society but rather its more stable representatives. A Presbyterian pastor of my acquaintance, though puzzled about the phenomena, stated that those who spoke in tongues were the most effective and respected members of his congregation. Glossolaliacs tend to be normal.

Another expression of conversion more visible today is the excellent program for alcoholics carried on by Alcoholics Anonymous. The techniques of conversion were derived from Buchmanism, modified to fit the needs of alcoholics. The well known Twelve Steps of AA include first a kind of conviction of sin; in other words, a recognition that one is hopelessly ill and cannot help himself. Then comes the acknowledgement, even if merely on trial, that there is a Higher Power who can help, and finally the willingness to help others, which implements that follow-up and discipline in which the alcoholic comes to help himself.

Bill W., one of the founders of AA, told me of the spiritual experience which saved him from drink. He was in a hospital room, where he was told that his only hope of being saved from drink was to remain locked up for the rest of his life. An alcoholic friend who had been enabled to control his urges through the

Oxford Group told him of the power of religion to save him. Shortly afterward, there ensued a powerful religious experience in which, as he told me, his hospital room seemed to be bathed in a heavenly light, and the conviction came to him that he was going to be able to control his drinking. Subsequent to his release, and even after AA had been started, there had been many temptations both to discouragement and to drink. But whenever he called his experience to mind, he knew that he could stay away from drink and that AA would eventually be successful. Once again we find the hints of a pattern familiar in conversion. First comes the conviction of failure or "hitting bottom" in the case of the alcoholic, then the surrender to a force that seems greater than oneself leading to an access of ecstatic power and the fresh feelings of confidence and joy of the "new birth." Then finally there is the slow, often tedious, consolidating of the new life through disciplined living and contact with others requiring courage, fortitude, and will.

MYSTICISM

Since there was a suggestion of mysticism in the light that bathed the hospital room of Bill W., his case makes a good transition for us to what seems to be the most captivating and transforming of all the experiences commonly open to man, namely the mystical state. This seems broader in its application than conversion, which may be a conversion to a very narrow conception of truth if not even demonic forms of it. The conversion of many Germans to Nazism before the last war, for example, had many quasireligious elements of an ecstatic variety in them. This is not to say that the power of mysticism itself may not be deflected to demonic uses. Aldous Huxley's *Grey Eminence* (1966), a study of Father Joseph, Cardinal Richelieu's secretary of state, is an account of an undoubted mystic whose dogmatic position and involvement with the manipulation of power led to his becoming the most hated man in Europe. But most characteristically, mysticism leads to compassion and a wider view of human nature that resists compartmentalization and restrictions.

As with conversion, mystical experience leads to a change of values usually characterized by a heightening of interest in the nonrational aspects of consciousness experienced in ecstasy. By providing a focus, this usually improves the integration of personality and forms a base for higher forms of growth. Examples from history of this type of change of personality in well-known mystics following mystical ecstasy include Gautama the Buddha, also called the Compassionate; Socrates, whose enlightenment Plato reflected in the Allegory of the Cave in *The Republic;* Saint Francis, whose sympathy with both animals and men is well known; Pascal the French mathematician, whose change of interests in the direction of religion was accelerated after the date of his ecstasy; George Fox, the Founder of Quakerism. In our own day, Arthur Koestler's devotion to Communism began to lessen after his mystical experience in prison and turned toward increased respect for religion and democracy (Koestler, 1955). In the mystical experiences triggered by psilocybin in the Good Friday experiment mentioned in my first lecture, Dr. Walter Pahnke discovered that those students reporting mystical experience also reported greater involvement with people and more significant religious lives in the six months following the experiment (Clark, 1969, pp. 77-80).

Since the meaning of the term "mysticism" is so elusive, those who use the term often confuse other people with their own vague conceptions of that of which they are speaking. They tend either to use the word as a term of opprobrium or an equally general expression of approval. The Good Friday experiment is not only the only thorough scientifically designed study known to me in the field of mysticism, but also it definitely pointed in the direction of improved personal functioning following mystical ecstasy. This clarity was possible due to two things. First, Pahnke started with a clear-cut definition of mysticism based mostly on Stace. Then he had at his disposal reasonably reliable triggers of the mystical state in the form of well-motivated and prepared theological students, a favoring environment including sympathetic guides; and a tool in the form of a drug to set the ecstasy in motion. The experiment helps us to a better understanding of the wholesome effects of their experiences on the personalities of the great mystics. Furthermore, it supports the speculations of Stace that mysticism, through its traditionally recognized capacity to generate compassion and love, is certainly *one* of the sources of human ethics and may possibly be their *only* and *true* source (Stace, 1961, Chap. 8).

Though not as rigorously as Pahnke, I have found confirmation of his results in a questionnaire I have circulated among 100 unselected users of LSD-type drugs mentioned in my first chapter. Most of these had taken the drugs under conditions which I would deplore, yet only one wished he had not taken them. There was *not a single one* who did not report at least *some* of the characteristics linked with mysticism. Consequently, it is significant that 82 per cent reported an increase in their sympathies and compassion. At the very least, these results point to stirrings of a very profound level of consciousness and toward the power of the mystical consciousness, a power worthy of the claims made in behalf of religion that it is the pillar, support, and source of all ethics and goodness.

THE MODERN COUNTERCULTURE

Despite the dubiousness and dangers of the drug culture, I have been particular in referring to the psychedelic drugs (to be distinguished from other varieties of drugs), since I believe we can learn much by studying their effects carefully and critically. They are certainly an important element in the religious movement among our youth, which I see as the most dynamic expression of religion of our times. In their rebellion against the established traditions of middle-class America, many youth have gone far beyond the churches in their pursuit not only of the mystical values of the East but also of these same values embedded in the mystical traditions of the West, and probably, as I believe, in all of human nature. It is on this probability, and on this probability alone, that we can rest any hope there is of building a new and harmonious world. From such a vantage point, religious experience takes on an importance far beyond that of a mere academic or religious exercise.

Yet the hippies in their "green rebellion" would seem a slender reed on which to base any hope for a better world. Youth in revolt

against their elders are too ready to reject tradition and the
wisdom of the ages. Drug-using communes like the Manson family
would seem like the very reverse of that on which any kind of
stable base could be founded, unless it were a demonic one.
Perhaps one thing that has to be said about the counterculture and
the hippie movement is that it is often confused.

This, it must be admitted, is one of the shortcomings of the
contemporary cult of youth. Many of the hippies *are* confused, if
for no other reason than the fact that in their rejection of reason
and the social structures of their parents, they tend to reject that
part of the collaborative team of the rational and the nonrational
that supplies guidance, structure, and criticism. But on the other
hand, they tend to supply that vitality, power, and energy that
radically can change human nature.

How can we say that this is so? Their human nature does not
seem to be changed but only bent on what they themselves
celebrate as "tuning in, turning on, and dropping out." Almost as
by common consent, we of the older generation brand this sort of
thing as escape. The use of drugs seems only to underline this
interpretation. There is no doubt that one can select examples that
will support this case.

But one can also support the case for the exact opposite — that
these young people have somehow sensed deeply within themselves a basic hunger for that which will make some sense of their
lives. This hunger goes much deeper and is more pervasive than the
desire for drugs, which most come to realize are not ends in
themselves but simply one means to awaken in some persons a
perception of a larger world. Many youth are either not interested
in the drugs or have gone beyond them to other methods of
achieving the same thing. The interest in meditation, in Zen, in
other Eastern forms of religious disciplines, in new experimental
forms of Christian worship tinged with encounter methodology
along with ecstatic celebration symbolized by the appearance of
the guitar and the talk of love — all point to these deeper, mystical
forms of religion of which I have been speaking. In Judaism we are
hearing more of Hasidism, while some young people are even
reviving interest in Sufism, the Muslim mystical tradition.

Along with these activities, some of them faddish and

superficial but others deeply sincere, there go the radical changes of values that so often is seen in the mystics. For long years many of us have gone to church and been told to lay not up treasures on earth where moth doth corrupt and thieves break through and steal. Our ready assent to such pious sentiments, nevertheless, hardly ever carry over into any kind of effective action. The reaction that most of us have to treasure upon earth is that we are not enabled to lay up half enough of it. It is the hippies and the Zen enthusiasts who, after an overwhelming encounter with what they themselves will identify as beauty, ultimate reality, or the Holy, will reject the crass, materialistic values of middle-class culture. Forsaking all, many of them, even if not point by point following scriptural instruction, have in effect come too close to the spirit of Christ's teaching for their parents to feel quite comfortable about it.

But there is no doubt that for many of our youth, their religious experiences have marked a sharp and visible break with the kind of lives in which they have grown up. This has come largely from their change in values perceived through mysticism, however achieved. Success, competition, college degrees, getting ahead, acquiring the status symbols of prosperity — all of these things have taken a lower rank in their scale of values. The bizzarrely festive clothing of the hippies are largely messages to their middle-class parents that they have discarded the old values of neatly trimmed respectability. Through the smoking of marijuana or the use of stronger psychedelics they have been introduced to experiences of beauty and religious depth which they may not know what to do with but which they feel their parents would never understand. This is the explanation of many runaways and the reason why there are hundreds of communes or extended family groups to be found in city and country throughout the land. (For an account of representative communes, see reference to Hedgepeth, Stock, and to Houriet in the first lecture.)

It is in these communes that one can see most visibly the changes in behavior that have been brought about through modern religious experience. You must not get the idea from my references to drugs that these communes are all devoted to continuing drug use. Many have given it up and forbid the use of drugs within the community. But the great majority of residents have at least tried the drugs and have found an opening to vast reaches of inner space and the beginning of a spiritual quest that will take many of them far beyond the drugs. As one "graduate" of drug use put it, the drugs supply a door to a new life but not a room to live in. This generalization, however, might be applied to nearly all forms of religious experience.

Many of these communities have collapsed when faced with some of the realities of self support and the maintenance of personal relations. The life with like-minded idealists that in summer weather seemed so attractive may lose its appeal under winter's blasts when living together harmoniously becomes an achievement rather than a pleasant holiday. Also, neighbors and the police have often proved inhospitable, particularly when the commune has not developed some sense of responsibility for those around them, as indeed some of the more stable communities have done. Those that have survived have learned that they could not do without a modicum of the organization they despised in "the Establishment," while rejected middle-class cleanliness is found a necessity if communities are to avoid crippling illnesses and epidemics. In other words, just as ecstasy requires the structure supplied to it by the rational, so does the transcendental community require the support of organization and hard work if the communes are to become the monastic movement of the twentieth century, as has been suggested.

But the point I am making is that for many youth there has been a radical break with their past lives and their families that has been far from a fad with all of them. Their religious experiences have given them some taste of that sympathy and warmth of fellowship that we call love, and they have set out whether with their friends or with the strangers within their gates, to meditate, to experiment, and to find those spiritual exercises that will lead them toward a more significant existence than they have observed among their elders.

The rise of this counterculture raises many questions but none of more importance to the churches than what its final disposition is to be religiously. To the extent that it is only a passing fad, it can be dismissed, like the flowers with which the hippies adorn their hats, as a phenomenon that is here today and gone tomorrow. On the other hand, there are many who, like Timothy Leary, are ready to be harrassed and imprisoned rather than to renounce what to them are the means through which they approach God. Leary's former colleague, Richard Alpert, now called Baba Ram Dass and graduated from drug use, has joined a Hindu spiritual community on the slopes of the Himalyas in India and has a sizable following in this country. Such people constitute the hard core of this modern monasticism, and any movement with a hard core capable of such devotion is bound to have an impact. I have attended a service led by Baba Ram Dass at a Unitarian church in Boston with pews filled and young people crowded on the floors. Alternatively, they listened attentively to remarks of religious wisdom and to songs accompanied by the sitar, then chanted, then meditated in perfect silence. It is this kind of religious dynamic which the churches can ill afford to lose.

It cannot be said that expressions of youth's interest in religious experience have had no influence on the churches, but in general a youth's visit to his church or synagogue will impress on him more sharply what he has already sensed as the generation gap. For the most part, however, the type that will hear Ram Dass or Timothy Leary will not otherwise bother even to step inside the churches. Yet these youth have nearly as much need of the church as the church has need of them with their hunger for celebration and their acquaintance with the nonrational. The Roman Catholic Bishop Cletus O'Donnell of Madison, Wisconsin, commenting on the gap between younger and older members of the Church, observed, "It is certainly curious that many young people are searching out the mystical and the sacred and do not find it in their churches" (1970). It is probable that many who run the churches have either never known profound religious experience or, if they have, have forgotten it.

Let me try to put what I have said in perspective by telling you the story of a runaway Italian kid named Frank. Perhaps I might preface the story by asking you what the average American small village would think of a visit from Jesus and his twelve disciples. Would they be arrested as vagrants or just invited to leave town?

I read the story of Frank in a psychiatric publication in an account of hippies in San Francisco (Allen and West, 1968, p. 369).

> Frank was a real cool guy — he grooved on trees, on birds, and on people. But his parents were worried and embarrassed. They had worked hard and now had a good life, and here Frank was running around with a bunch of dropouts. He didn't bathe too often, he went barefoot, he even panhandled for food.
>
> Finally Frank was discovered breaking into his father's warehouse and giving things out free — the first Digger store. His old man took him to court. In a fit of pique, Frank stripped off his clothes, threw them at his father's feet, and stomped out of the courtroom, stark naked. Well, Frank didn't run away to Haight-Ashbury, for there was no San Francisco then, but he has become a patron saint to the hippies . . . .

For that is the story of the person *after whom* San Francisco was named!

CONCLUSION

In these lectures I have been writing of what I see to be the essential psychological principles of religion: the relationship between the rational and the nonrational and the importance of conversion, religious ecstasy, and the mystical consciousness, all of which may have such profound influence on men's attitudes and behavior. But I would like to end by sounding an even broader note.

Within recent history we have seen at least five widespread revolutions in Western history: the American Revolution, the French Revolution, the Russian Revolution, the Nazi Revolution, and the Indian Revolution. All of them started with a considerable amount of idealism but ended with much less of it.

Only the religions of the world have shown an institutional durability that has carried them through millenia. Even so, their histories have been very checkered and their paths by no means smooth. But that they should have persisted as long as they have speaks for some secret of the human soul that, continuously reviving itself, pours back sources of life-giving strength into worn-out institutional frames.

The conclusion I am proposing here is that this source of strength is needed at this stage in human history more desperately than ever before. For we now have under man's direction a source of destruction so terrible that it is hard to see how any conflict could start in earnest without devastating most of what we call the civilized world. We are told that man is too intelligent to let such a war begin. Everyone knows that war leaves everyone worse off than before.

Yet, despite all of our intelligence, as we look on the precarious belances of the "cold war," it is hard to see the nations of the earth getting closer together. We note the same old crises of power politics, and if we apply hard-headed logic, it is hard to escape the conviction that sooner or later there will be an explosion, maybe the final one.

The suggestion that I have to offer is that our only hope for a resolution of our differences is in some way to harness the religious consciousness to politics. I am not saying that all we need in order to solve our political problems are politicians with mystical experience. The situation calls for skills and capacities far more complex than merely that. All I am proposing is that without the wisdom, broad sympathies, and compassion that are rooted in mystical depth and flow from it, our task is hopeless. This is the quality that distinguishes the true statesman from the mere political leader. It is significant that the only modern revolution that left the contending parties with more respect for and ability to communicate with one another after the conflict than before was led by such a mystic-statesman. I am thinking of India's break from England under Ghandi. And the one quality that sets Lincoln clearly above others in our roster of presidents is his compassion. Furthermore, in *The Republic,* Plato insisted that only those who were capable of enlightenment, like his master Socrates, should be entrusted with the guidance of the State.

Yet in seeking for religious leadership among our heads of state, we must be careful that we define it properly. The addition of religious motives to national policies in the past has only made ensuing wars more merciless and demonic. Doubtless this has been the case because these wars were facilitated through that which we are assured today is going to save us from war, namely reason and the creature of reason — dogma. I am not proposing here that we discard reason but that it needs to be informed and enlightened by that which every great religious leader has somehow derived from his religious experience and in some way uttered. This is a broad human sympathy and compassion, the fruit of the mystical consciousness, through which alone man may sense immediately the unity of all things and all creatures, and the brotherhood of man.

I take it that this is the message the poet was trying to express in one of our most perceptive hymns, in which Clifford Bax calls us from our obsessions with the false and limited shapes of things and power, those instruments of temporality and death, to an awareness of the ultimate realities, those fruits of religious experience that last and endure. It is only when we become aware of such realities that we are truly awake. The true dreamers are the power politicians and conquerors who in ages past have drenched the pages of history with blood, pursuing a perfect security that has always eluded them. The "hard-headed realists" of today continue to preach peace but to insist on those things they cannot have without war. Ahead of us looms a brooding holocaust that neither mere intelligence, idealism, nor an outward religious thrust without roots will be able to avert. We are walking in our sleep thinking that the everyday realities are the ultimate ones. This is the poet's message, and though not part of my psychological analysis, it is this conviction that has made it seem worthwhile to me to present this brief psychological review of religious experience of these past three lectures. Let me end these lectures with a few lines from the hymn "Turn Back, O Man" (Bax).

> Earth might be fair and all men glad and wise.
> Age after age their tragic empires rise,
> Built while they dream, and in that dreaming weep;
> Would man but wake from out his haunted sleep,
> Earth might be fair and all men glad and wise.

REFERENCES

Allen, J. P. and West, L. J.: Flight from violence: Hippies and the green rebellion. American Journal of Psychiatry, 1968, 125, (3), 364-370. (quotation on p. 56 used by permission of authors and American Journal of Psychiatry).

Anonymous: Alcoholics Anonymous. New York, Works Publishing Co., 1941.

Clark, W. H.: The psychology of religion. New York, Macmillan, 1958.

Clark, W. H.: Chemical ecstasy: Psychedelic drugs and religion. New York, Sheed & Ward, 1969.

Gerlach, L. P. and Hine, V. H.: Pentecostals growth. Journal for the Scientific Study of Religion, 1968, 7, (1), 23-40.

Goodman, F.: Phonetic analysis of glossolalia in four cultural settings. Journal for the Scientific Study of Religion, 1969, 8, (2), 227-239.

Hine, V. H.: Pentecostal glossolalia: Toward a functional interpretation. Journal for Scientific Study of Religion, 1969, 8, (2), 211-226.

Huxley, A.: Grey eminence. New York, Harper & Row, 1966.

James, William: The varieties of religious experience. New York, New American Library, 1958.

Koestler, A.: The Invisible Writing. Boston, Beacon Press, 1955.

O'Donnell, Cletus: In The New York Times, December 5, 1970.

Sargant, W.: The battle for the mind. Baltimore, Penguin books, 1961.

Chapter 4

PSYCHOLOGIZED RELIGION:
ITS EGOCENTRIC PREDICAMENT
A Theologian's Point of View

JAMES DAANE

THE inclusion of a School of Psychology within a seminary is unique. Its inclusion at Fuller Theological Seminary was justified by the conviction that the Christian Church is vitally concerned not only with the Gospel it preaches but also with the inner religious experience of those who believe or disbelieve it. The Church must not only be a proclaimer of the Gospel; it must also be a pastor of souls.

The legitimacy of this dual concern with the object of its proclamation, the Gospel, and with the subjective, personal believing response to the Gospel is reflected in the biblical use of the term "faith." In biblical usage, the term faith defines both the believing response to the Gospel and that content of the Gospel which is believed, as in the biblical clause, "the faith once for all delivered to the saints." It is also reflected in the biblical language which asserts that the Christian response is a faith in the "faithfulness of God." Therefore, the act of believing, and that which is believed, are distinguishable but not separable. Not only are they inseparable, but in biblical thought the object of faith (the Gospel) shapes the nature of the human believing response. Faith as a human response to the Gospel, consequently, cannot be understood or served without a knowledge of the Gospel. Thus psychology as a science of the human psyche and theology as the science of Gospel are vitally related.

Calvin, on a different level, reflected this kind of relationship when he discussed the knowledge of God and the knowledge of man. For Calvin, the right knowledge of God was prerequisite to a right knowledge of man. Thus while the former has priority over the latter, the former, nevertheless, has no independent existence apart from the latter. A right knowledge of God, the object, carries with it a right knowledge of man, the subject. Similarly, as regards psychology and theology, the religious response and the object to which the response is made are related in such fashion that while what is believed does not, in fact, exist apart from a believer, the believer can only be understood in the light of what he believes. In the actual life of the Church, this relationship is reflected in the way in which the Church understands its task. The Church must not only administer the Word; it must also minister to the person. A minister of the Christian Church is both preacher and pastor, and he conceives of his pastoral task as shaped by the theological understanding of the Word he preaches.

This does not mean that theology dictates to psychology, or that theology teaches but does not learn from the psychologist. After all, theology, too, is only a science. It is the partial, fallible, never-completed reflection of the Church upon the divine Word. Theology no less that psychology operates under the norm of the Word of God.

Thus on the one hand, theology must learn from the other sciences in its efforts to correct and more fully achieve itself as a science. This includes the science of psychology. Since the act of believing reflects the faith which is believed, a psychological study of the believer can contribute to the correction and deepening of theology. On the other hand, since the Faith that is believed shapes the personal act of believing, an authentic religious psychology must draw upon Christian theology; understood is the Church's knowledge and understanding of the word of God. This is the only kind of psychology that can make a contribution both to theology and to the believer's religious health. Thus theology and psychology need each other and can each be helpful to the other. But each can render and receive such mutual help only as they increasingly understand their peculiar interrelationship and recognize the normative character of the Word.

Fuller Theological Seminary recognizes this peculiar relation-ship between theology and psychology, between the act of faith and the object of faith, and the dual task of the Church to articulate the biblical Faith and to engage in the care of souls. For obvious reasons, no seminary can require that its candidates for the ministry be graduates from a school of psychology. The best any seminary can do within its own curriculum is to give its students some training in pastoral care. Anyone admitted to Fuller's School of Psychology is required to undergo two years of theological training. This requirement rests on the conviction that there can be no authentic psychology of religion apart from Christian theology. Christian truth is an essential element in an authentic psychology of religion whether it concerns itself only with the psychology of Christian people, or with the psychology of the non-Christian as well.

The task of uncovering the relationship between theology and psychology is difficult and demanding, and far from being accomplished. The search for such an understanding of theology and psychology is no mere academic pursuit. It is of very considerable practical value and necessity. Unless it can in some real measure be achieved, no justification can be made for Fuller's inclusion of a School of Psychology, and the danger is real that a school of psychology loose of basic biblical principles would be detrimental to a theological seminary.

Walter Houston Clark is a prominent psychologist of religion. He is very sympathetic to religion and believes that religion in its essence is unique, a position he declares unpopular among his colleagues. By this he means, quite rightly, that religion cannot be explained by something else and thereby be reduced to a phenomenon of a different order. He holds that human life without religion is without meaning or value. And he confesses to be a Christian who holds that mysticism is the highest and most authentic form of religion. Such explicit, candid self-identification of who he is and where he stands bespeaks honesty and integrity.

But I am still left with the question of whether Dr. Clark's lectures really address themselves to the purpose of the Finch Symposium. The purpose is to uncover a closer relationship between theology and psychology. What we have, let it be frankly admitted, is little enough. Do we now have more? In my judgment, we do not. Such light and help as these lectures possess fall obliquely rather than directly on the goal of integrating theology and psychology. Dr. Clark's lectures clearly etch a tempting route that should not be taken. The failure of these lectures to move closer to this goal stems neither from Clark's personal integrity nor from his academic competence but from his chosen methodology.

How does Clark envisage and execute his task as a psychologist of religion? This is an easy question, for he himself is clearly aware and explicitly announces both his presuppositions and the methodology he employs in his pursuit of the psychological study of religion.

Clark declares that "religion in its essence is unique." By this he means that religion cannot be reduced to something of a different order or magnitude. Religion as a human experience is not simply another form of sex, for example, or of the anxiety of finitude, or of individual or social self-projection. Religion is a reality in its own right. It neither lives by the sufferance of something else, nor is susceptible to explanation in nonreligious concepts. With this one may agree. Yet unless one makes at this point some theological affirmations, such as that religion is a component of human nature as created in the divine image, religious experience remains vulnerable to be reduced to psychology and explicable in psychological concepts. As we shall see, Clark in the end internalizes religious experience and reduces it to a psychological state of awareness, thereby extending it to such a variety of human experiences that the uniqueness of religious experience is lost.

Clark rightly extends the uniqueness that characterizes religion as an irreducible phenomenon to all religions. But his presuppositions are such that he cannot recognize Christianity, either as an objective Faith or as a subjective experience, as something unique and distinctive from, say, Hinduism and Hindu religious experience. Nor can he allow that either Hinduism or any other religion has a unique unshared quality. Clark admits that he will merely "glance" at non-Christian religions but makes the admission apologetically, explaining it as a defect of his provincialism. If in his study of the psychology of religion he thinks and speaks more in the idiom of Christianity than, say, Hinduism, this he says is only because he has lived in a Christian rather than in a Hindu milieu.

Clark admits that his "whole approach" could be called phenomenological. Such an approach dictates that no religion, Christian or non-Christian, can be regarded as unique. With this, all theology, and all possibilities of theological affirmations, are ruled out from the beginning. By his method, in all outer space, theology and psychology would never dock.

Clark also tells us that as a psychologist of religion he has no intention of giving us a "Christian apologetic." And he does not regard this as an exercise of personal options. A Christian apologetic he says would not be "appropriate to my task." He then defines his task as he sees it: "I am a social scientist, and any scientist is concerned with observing his field dispassionately and reporting what he sees there." His task then is defined as merely observing and reporting religious experience. Evaluation of religious experience and the defense of Christian or Hindu religious experience over against any other kind of religious experience is regarded as outside his task. This is supported by the assertion that "there is not a Christian psychology of religion to be distinguished from any other." He is, therefore, on his own admission, "not a student of Christian psychology."

The term "Christian psychology" is, of course, an ambiguous and muddy term. Yet what Clark means by it is clear. In his usage, it means that Christianity as an objective Faith and as a subjective religious experience has no special or unique role in religious psychology. He says it all when he asserts, "I am not a student of Christian psychology but a psychologist who happens to be a Christian." The fact that he happens to be a Christian has nothing to do with the manner in which he pursues the study of religious psychology. On this approach, it is understandable that he disclaims the role of Christian apologete, or Hindu apologete, for that matter. It is also understandable that he is unwilling to make any distinctions in kind between Christian religious experience and Hindu religious experience; between the Christian's experience of the God who is the father of Jesus Christ and the Hindu's experience of his God; between the peace that Paul found and that which the alcoholic finds through Alcoholic Anonymous; between the Christian mystic's experience of God and that of the LSD's self-induced experience of God.

In Clark's approach, it is also understandable that the Object of religious experience can go nameless. Nameless not indeed, as Clark suggests, in the tradition of Christian mysticism where God is regarded as ultimately beyond all naming but in the sense that it matters not whether God is the Yahweh of Israel, the Buddha of India, or the Zeus of the Greeks. Clark's God is essentially nameless, not because He is greater than his revelation as the Christian mystics held, but since there is no unique revelation of God, any name attributed to God by man is as valid or invalid as any other.

At any rate, this much is clear: If there is no "Christian psychology of religion to be distinguished from any other," and if one's religious psychology is not affected by whether one "happens to be a Christian" or happens not to be one, then it is surely clear that psychology has nothing to do with Christian theology. Every theological presupposition about religion and religious experience, and every usage of theological norms in religious psychology is an unwarranted encroachment of theology upon the field of psychology.

Given his chosen theological presuppositions and his methodology determined by them, Clark's religious psychology, by definition, could not directly contribute to Fuller Seminary's venture of faith: i.e. a better understanding of the relationship between theology and psychology. Clark's methodological cards were stacked against this realization.

Nonetheless, these lectures may contribute significantly in an indirect movement toward this goal of a greater understanding of how theology and psychology are related. I say "may" because a "will" depends upon how perceptively we read and understand his lectures. One thing seems very clear to me. For all his theoretical insistence that the study of the psychology of religion must stay free from theology, Clark, in the actual doing of religious psychology, himself brings significant theological factors into play and gives them quite decisive roles in his religious psychology. As we shall see later, at the most crucial points, he violates his own concept of religious psychology, ceases to be a mere dispassionate social scientist-reporter, and himself becomes a preacher of the only religion which provides hope for our world.

But first we must consider how religious matters are shaped and emerge from the mold of Clark's religious psychology. Consideration shall first be given to religion as mysticism, then to conversion.

RELIGION AS MYSTICISM

Mysticism, asserts Clark, is the essence, and therefore the most authentic expression, of religion. This conclusion is dictated by his methodology. Religious experience, according to Clark, is what religious psychology studies. As a psychologist, Clark is ultimately concerned with only what occurs within a man's skin. Since what happens religiously within Chrisitan, Hindu, Buddhist, Taoist, etc., and even within the one-time alcoholic, current drug user, etc., takes various forms of human experience, Clark, as a scientist, does not in fact report dispassionately what he observes, but rather, as every scientist must, searches for what is common in these varied internal experiences. What he comes up with is this: all have an internal experience of some Reality that exists beyond the boundaries of their own skin. This is the essence of the religious experience: a skin-bound, vague experience of some Reality external to and beyond one's self. Clark asks a psychological question and thereby gets a psychological answer. Men have an internal experience within themselves of something beyond themselves. This, says Clark, on theological, nonpsychological grounds, is a *religious* experience. Since such religious experience of something more than the self occurs internally, within the skin of the subject of such experience, such religion is judged to be mysticism.

Clark is right in his understanding of mysticism (though he misunderstands Christian mysticism which inconsistently paid more attention to Christ than Clark does.) With his presuppositions, Clark is quite consistent in almost wholly ignoring Christ.

The distinctive feature of mysticism is the belief that man, within the boundaries of his skin, within the limits of his own inner experience, can come into contact with God. Thus mysticism, as Clark urges, lies within the potentiality of every man. The mystic, to make contact with God, needs nothing external to his own skin; he needs no Christ of history, an external Bible, nor a historical Church, nor another man as missionary of the Gospel. Clark's brand of non-Christian mysticism does not require a God who meets the mystic in history. It may be enough if the mystic is confronted by Alcoholics Anonymous. Such a confrontation, according to Clark, can effect an authentic mystical experience. Such an experience does not require the presence of God in a Jesus of Nazareth. It can be effected by the moral force of Alcoholics Anonymous. Even such a concrete historic confrontation is not however, required. An authentic mystical experience of God can be achieved by the man who takes a trip, perhaps drug induced, deep into primitive resources of his own instincts.

In Christian thought, man meets God outside of himself in the form of historic Christ, Scripture, Church, preacher, missionary; accordingly, a man serves God by serving those who exist outside of his own skin and experience.

For Clark, however, religious psychology is concerned with an interior religious experience, and only such an interior experience is authentically religious. What about the Christian's out-of-his skin, external actions in everyday life? What about his religious experience which consists in serving others in love, feeding the hungry, visiting the sick and the fatherless?

Here Clark is ambivalent and unclear. On the one hand, he defines authentic religion as mystical, something within the dimensions of the interior life of man and God. Since God does not meet him outside his skin, true response to, and service of, God occurs within his private internal relationship to God. Religious activity is properly regarded as an internal experience between God and the human soul. This motif leads Clark to assert that he "in a secondary or even tertiary sense might admit certain activities to be religious."

Are feeding the hungry, working for the Church, preaching the gospel, praying for others, witnessing to non-Christians, confessing Jesus Christ before the Church and the world, religious activities? According to Clark, in a secondary or even tertiary way, "we might admit" them to be religious. Clark's language indicates how extremely difficult it is for him to admit that any action a Christian performs for others, whether God or man, is authentically religious. He is basically committed to the position that true religion is only a mystical "inner experience of the Holy." On hearing this side of Clark's view of internal mystical religion and his depreciation of Christian action, one would never expect to see Clark feed the hungry or march in a civil rights demonstration. Yet who knows? For he also insists that "every act and attitude of man" can be religious if it is sufficed with the warmth and compassion that are the mystical fruits of an experience with the Holy. Thus no act can be regarded in the first instance as distinctively religious, yet every act induced by an experience of the Holy suffused by a warming flow and compassion can be, not in a secondary or tertiary way, but in a primary sense, an act of authentic religious experience. Clark illustrates this point by citing the Hindu's reaction to the cobra!

Operating within the limitations of his methodology, Clark reduces religion and religious experience to a mysticism which is independent of anything in history and can break out of its skin to enter history in religious action only by violating its own premises.

A limitation of religious experience which includes the internal ecstatic experiences but excludes religious activity as a part of religious experience is an arbitrary limitation, which in Clark's case is the consequence of his chosen method of doing religious psychology. Clark has gotten himself caught in the ego-centric predicament.

This entrapment also appears in Clark's discussion of the Object of religious experience. Except for pure illusions, experience is always an experience of something. For Clark, this something cannot be an Object that has met man and disclosed himself in history. This is ruled out by the insistence that religion is an inner mystical ecstatic experience. An ecstatic experience is, by definition, one in which the self stands outside himself. He gets outside of his own skin. But does Clark's religious mystic actually have an ecstatic experience? It would seem not, for his religious mystic at his highest moment of experience is left with simply a sense or awareness of its Object. He is, says Clark, open to the transcendent. The Object is never seized; it never becomes *my* God. In the ecstatic mystical experience, the Object is never possessed by our knowledge so that one can say "I know God." The mystical experience, according to Clark, does not include knowledge of the Object experienced; it leaves the religious person with merely subjective feelings of love, compassion, and brotherhood — the recognition and acceptance, not of God, but of other men.

Presuppositions that dictate a methodology which in turn dictates the reduction of religious experience to what can occur only within the self can at best have an objective religious referent about which ultimately nothing can be said. The Object of Clark's mysticism remains so much in the dark, unknown, that it is only by its pragmatic tests, its fruits, as Clark puts it, that determination can be made of whether it is divine or demonic. For Clark, the psychologist, it makes little, if any, difference whether the Object experienced is called God, the Unknown, the Holy Terror (Otto's *mysterium tremendum),* no-God, or something else. Clark appeals to the language of the Christian mystics who have described God as the "dazzling darkness," "dark silence," the "void," the "full void," the "wayless path," the "teeming desert."

Given these definitions of the Object of ecstatic mystical religious experience, it comes as no surprise that the experience is described as unutterable and ineffable. This flows from the correspondence between the experience and the object of the experience.

Clark's mysticism is obviously not a Christian mysticism, and this raises the question of whether his appeal to Christian mystics is not too facile. There has indeed been a strain of mysticism in the Christian Church. But there are mystics and mystics. Paul had a mystical experience, St. Teresa and Dutch John Van Ruysbroeck were Christian mystics, but they thought themselves going beyond, but not denying, the reality and knowledge of God disclosed in the person and history of Jesus Christ.

An experience of any object is in part shaped and determined by the nature of the object. The only exception is pure illusion, of which there can be no science. If the Object of religious mystical experience, and no less the experience itself, remains a blur against a shadowy, undefinable background, the question arises whether these data are amenable to scientific investigation and whether such religious psychology is really psychology or simply the musings of an individual ploring over data of his own psyche.

CONVERSION

The features of Clark's psychology emerge clearly in his discussion of conversion. His earlier interest in conversion, he says, gave way to an intense interest in mystical experience. The mystical experience has richer possibilities and represents a "riper and more penetrating form of spiritual awakening and growth." This, declares Clark, stems from the fact that the mystical experience occurs at a deeper level of human personality than does conversion. Mystical experience occurs at a level of personality even deeper than that of the unconscious. Conversion and mysticism are, however, related. And of the two types of conversion, the gradual and the sudden-abrupt, Clark prefers the latter because it springs from the more primitive impulses of the human psyche.

Conversion, and in an even profounder sense, mystical experience, it is claimed, involve a durative change of personality: living for a new set of values, a radical break with one's past life. No Christian can object to these psychological descriptions of conversion, but Clark objects when these purely formal psychological descriptions are employed normatively to determine what human experiences are and are not conversion experiences. Lacking all theological content, they are sufficiently elastic to cover whatever the psychologist decides to call conversion. Since the Object of conversion or the mystic experience is vaguely described, and since the deepest origin of the conversion experience lies in the most primitive instincts of the human psyche, the conversion experience that occurs between them is so loosely defined as to cover whatever Clark decides to designate as a conversion. The changes effected by Alcoholics Anonymous, by snake handlers, by drugs, by German conversion to Nazism, by chemically induced ecstasy, by Wesley's proclamation of hell, by massive physical exhaustion − all come within the category of conversion. Such a theologically uncritical psychological extension of conversion is of little help to the serious Christian theologian striving to relate theology and psychology. Nor will we find comfort when Clark suggests that an exhausted and worn-down state of the human spirit achieved through various psychical and psychological techniques which make the psyche vulnerable to the conversion experience is what Jesus perhaps meant when he spoke of the little children who enter the Kingdom. And we are as little comforted by Clark's allusion to the parable of the sower to show that the conversion comes in many forms. The parable, in fact, shows rather that there are inauthentic as well as authentic experiences of conversion.

Given Clark's understanding of conversion, it can occur in any form and in any context. It can occur within the religious context of any religion and can indeed, as he suggests, occur in a no-God atheistic context. Any change of life, any redirection of life toward a new set of values, any experience that puts the inner life of man more together, is regarded as a conversion. The mere biological and unavoidable change of youth into old age induces the kind of new set of values which Clark calls conversion. A Western man's experience of learning to look at a cobra in the way a Hindu does would be a conversion, and if it should slither down deeper into his more primitive impulses it would thereby be enriched as an experience of the Holy. The fact that Clark happens to be a Christian has no deterring effect upon his definition of conversion and mystical experience. Providing no Christian apologetic by intention and devoid of all theological criteria by decision, Clark has deprived himself as a *psychologist* of the ability to detect any essential distinction between Paul's conversion to Jesus Christ and the Western man's new perspective on a cobra. By this route, the Christian committed to Christian theology and pursuing psychology is not inched along toward his goal of uncovering their interrelationships.

Some persons will doubtless be shocked by Clark's careful use of drugs to open up a person to an ecstatic experience of God (by whatever name). But if the blessings of conversion can, as Clark thinks, be induced by the use of drugs, what Christian would not, in view of the value of conversion, regard the results as warranting the method? Unless, of course, the drug-induced conversion is not an authentic conversion to God. But this judgment could only be made by recourse to the criteria of theology.

One additional comment: it would seem reasonable to expect a psychologist of religion, especially if he happens to be a Christian, to pay some serious attention to the psychology of the man who is converted, not by drugs or snake handlers, but by the hearing of the Church's proclamation of the gospel. The closest Clark comes to this is in his comments about Wesley's preaching of hell.

Clark says he is glad that Methodists no longer require converstion as a requirement of church membership. Aside from the limited factual truthfulness, it is interesting to observe why he is glad about this. The coercion of required conversion for church membership, he says, leads people to fake conversions. One wonders whether the requirement should have indeed been given up, since there are now so many ways to induce conversions and since they are by Clark's own evaluation of real religious value, being one long step toward the ineffable ecstatic experience of God. One is also left to wonder whether drug-induced conversion and mystical experiences are likely to insure a higher percentage of authentic conversions than an earlier Methodism was able to achieve.

I share Clark's concern that religion loses its transcendent dimension by being secularized into a mere activism and by the illusion that science, thought to govern all and control all, deprives men of an openness to the reality of God. For he is surely correct in his insistence that human life without religion deprives life of all that makes it meaningful and worth the candle.

I especially appreciate his recognition of the limitation of reason and his strong emphasis that religion, while not irrational, is more than rational. Religion without passion is indeed a bucket of ice. Where religion is regarded as wholly rational, there is no more room within religion for pathos than there is in a logical syllogism. Nor is there room in a wholly rational religion for religious ecstatic experience and, for that matter, for the symbolic, the poetic, or the tears of love. To insist that religion is not irrational is not to insist that it is wholly rational. Religion contains, as Clark rightly insists, that which is more than rational. And it will thus ever be as long as love is something more and other than rationality.

What the rational and what the ecstatic more-than-rational mean to Clark's thought is, of course, reflected in his understanding of religion as mysticism. The question then arises what reason means for Clark or, more precisely, what is the content of his practical reason that must, according to him, evaluate and guide the mystical religious experience. Clark wants rationality to serve a practical function within religious experience. But his rationality seems purely formal and empty. It appears to be without the content necessary to decide whether it is really practical and whether it is really a requirement of mysticism to make peace with the cobra and give it residence under one's roof. Nor does Clark's rationality appear to have the content necessary to determine what is a fake, and what is an authentic, experience of the Religious Object (however described or indescribable); or, if he were so inclined, to distinguish between a Christian and a non-Christian type of religious conversion.

Clark seems to insist on the more-than-rational in order to retain the openness required for the mystical experience, and to insist upon the rational in order to keep an ecstatic mysticism from being wholly irrational or even demonic. But neither his rationality nor his rationality-plus seems to have enough content to keep the other in balance. In Christian thought, the Scriptures present the normative content for both rationality and its practical function in religion and for the more-than-rational ecstatic element of religion. It is therefore capable of making a basic distinction between making peace with God and peace with a cobra; or between a Christian and a non-Christian conversion or experience of God. Clark's mysticism is incapable of making such distinctions and is therefore incapable of distinguishing between the fake and the authentic, though he himself admits the reality of the faked and the real within the mysticism which he proffers as the very essence of religion.

If the Object known and experienced in religious experience dictates the terms of its knowledge and experience capability, and the subject cannot be cut out of his experience of knowing the Object, then religion must always be more than rational. Clark's emphasis here is a wholesome one. It may well be that this is one of the most important things that theologians will learn from psychologists of religion. Theologians seem to have an almost congenital temptation to reduce the whole rich magnitude of religion into logical, rational patterns. Truth is reduced to religious propositions, and part of the religious life falls outside of them. If

Clark's mysticism has difficulty getting outside its own religious skin, theologians have long found history and religious experience elusive realities, though the Bible contains much of both. It is, therefore, no mere accident that systematic constructs of theology contain a substantial theology of human sin but no counterpart theologies of human love, compassion, or sense of unity and brotherhood — the very elements that constitute Clark's fruits of mysticism.

CONCLUSION

Every question has its direction and limits. Ask a psychological question and you will get a psychological, not a religious or theological, answer. Clark begins by setting theology — Christian or any other kind — aside. As a psychologist, he disowns the role of being an apologete for Christianity or any other religion. That he as a psychologist "happens to be a Christian" happens to mean that Christianity is not in any way normative for what he does as a psychologist. Nothing essential would be different for him as a psychologist if he happened to be a Hindu. Clark sees his task as a psychologist of religion as that of a "social scientist, and any scientist is concerned with observing his field dispassionately and reporting what he sees there."

How well does he succeed in these lectures in remaining true to his task as he sees it? Obviously not very well. He accepts the theology of no religion, Christian or non-Christian, as either directive or normative for his pursuit of the science of religious psychology. He defends no theology, no religion. Yet enroute to his scientific pursuit, he is all along developing a theology and religion of his own. In the name of psychology, he posits mysticism as the highest form of religion; and in the name of his theology of mysticism, he reduces all other religions to the same level and boldly proclaims that all religions are unique and that their uniqueness lies in the irreducibility of their ecstatic experience of some ineffable and indescribable transcendent reality. Clark demonstrates that a psychology without theology develops a theology of its own out of the psychological data it brings under its investigation.

How well does Clark remain true to his own definition of his task? As a scientist, he says he is "concerned with observing his field dispassionately and reporting what he sees there." Yet Clark not only becomes a theologican but also becomes an apologete who defends his mysticism and even becomes a preacher of it. He proposes mysticism as the only hope for our threatened world. Speaking about the cold war and the international crises of power politics, Clark asserts that "our only hope for a resolution of our differences is in some way to harness the religious consciousness to politics." And he adds that "without the wisdom, broad sympathies, and compassion that are rooted in the mystical depth and flow from it, our task is hopeless." And by "our task" he does not mean the task of the psychologist. He means the task of the psychologist and the rest of us to set the world straight. The "rest of us" would like to help, but those of us who are Christians would like to be in on the process of defining the task; and for Christians this would mean letting Christian theology be heard.

He further adds that the world "needs to be informed and enlightened" of that "broad human sympathy and compassion, the fruit of the mystical consciousness, through which alone man may sense immediately the unity of all things and all creatures, and the brotherhood of man." This is the voice of a preacher, not of a dispassionate psychologist. As a preacher and a teacher of preaching, I have no bias against preaching and can recognize preaching when I hear it. Clark's mystical consciousness projected as "our only hope" echoes the Church's proclamation of Jesus Christ as "our only hope." And his claim that through mysticism alone man may sense *immediately* the unity of all things, creatures, and the brotherhood of man is a reversal of the Christian claim of the unity of all things through the *mediation* of Jesus Christ. But it is preaching nonetheless — the voice of a prophet, not of a psychologist. The content is different, but the sound is the same.

Clark demonstrates that a psychology of religion which disowns theology generates its own, because without it, a study of the psychology of religion would be merely descriptive and thus meaningless. Students of the psychology of religion want to be, as Clark says, "useful." Indeed, on his first page, Clark says, "If you will forgive me the comparison with God ... in these three

lectures I hope most of all to be *used.*" But what is purely
phenomenological is not useful. Hence Clark adds theology — but
not traditional Christian theology.

Chapter 5

RELIGIOUS EXPERIENCE:
INCLUSIVE AND EXCLUSIVE
A Psychologist's Point of View

H. NEWTON MALONY

W HILE Clark's emphasis on the primacy of experience in religion is to be commended, he is, at one and the same
time, too exclusive and too inclusive in his discussions. He is too
exclusive in taking the position "that religion, in its essence, is
unique" and too inclusive in implying that social ethics flow
naturally out of mystical experiences. In contrast, it is herein
suggested that religious experience, while it may differ in content,
is nevertheless identical with other experience in terms of the
underlying processes involved. Further, it is herein suggested that
social ethics are of great complexity, and while they may issue
from moral sensitivity, they by no means are simple applications
of experience, as Clark implies.

Dittes (1968) suggested that the question of the qualitative
uniqueness of religious experience was the critical issue in the
psychology of religion. It is difficult to disagree with his assertion
that the psychological study of such experiences must be based on
the assumption that one is studying the same basic processes that
underlie all experience. To be sure, the experiencer judges his
experience to be different from the more mundane give and take
he has with persons and things in his environment. He often senses
the stimuli to which he is responding to be the revelations of a
personal God. But these aspects must not lead psychologists, as I
judge it led Clark, to endow the experience with essential
uniqueness, else we have no subject to study with the tools at our
disposal. The position that religious experience is essentially no
different from other experience can be taken without reducing
religion to psychology and/or questioning the validity of religious

assertions. William James (1908) was sensitive to these differences. The psychologist can still affirm that there may be more than his analysis allows him to say and accord other disciplines, such as theology, the privilege of handling such issues. That Clark was confused on this issue can be seen in his depreciation of the task of theology.

Clark's oversimplified view of social ethics is possibly based on his distrust of the rational in religion. This rational aspect, or dogma, is usually the product of the theologian's efforts. The constructs one brings to experiences help shape its meaning and effect just as much as the situation itself does. While this aspect of perception will be discussed in more detail later, suffice it to say that all religious experiences may not result in ethical behavior because the experiencer did not bring to the situation a set of interpretive constructs which included, e.g. a personal God who calls man into loving obedience and service to his fellowman. Tillich (1958) has discussed this type of difference in an article on types of healing. He suggested three possible interpretations of experience, i.e. natural, magical, and religious. As he interpreted it, a religious healing experience always included a dimension of encounter (with one's God) in which the believer felt he was made whole and should obediently serve God by loving his fellow man. Tillich was presuming the theological categories of the Jewish-Christian faith. Other religions may or may not include such ideas. Jung (1963) pointed out the basic difference between the self-reflected, introverted, a-ethical stance of much Eastern religion, and the outer directed, extroverted, ethical approach of Western religion, for example. There is no automatic ethical emission which comes from religious experience, per se, without the interpenetration of such previously held concepts which bring meaning to the experience. The Manson saga is but a glaring witness to this position.

The remainder of this essay will discuss these issues under four themes: one, the importance of constructs in interpreting experiences; two, the development and use of religious constructs; three the validity of induced religious experience; and four, the new demand for experience in religion. These themes could be interpreted as a basis affirmation of Clark's position of the primacy of the nonrational with the correctives noted above.

THE IMPORTANCE OF CONSTRUCTS
IN INTERPRETING EXPERIENCES

Constructs, where they are used to interpret experience, are based on the processes of sensation, perception, and response. While there is general agreement with the Lockean dictum that the mind is a blank tablet on which experience writes, the earlier notions (of a passive brain provoked to action by sensations received through sense organs on which the environment has impinged) have given way to a more complex model in which the brain is seen as very active. Thus experience is due just as much to that which the person lets affect him as to the situation itself. Wundt was sensitive to this through his construct of the "apperceptive mass" which persons bring into the present from out of the past. Further, Bruner (1956) has proposed a construct called "gating" to account for the fact that the mind screens what it lets in. Finally, Helson (1964), among other contemporary theorists in perception, sees the human being as a complex space-time averaging machine which constantly responds differentially to focal, background, and residual stimuli. Kelly (1955) applied this theory to interpersonal relations and suggested each man was a "scientist" in that he collected facts, made hypotheses, then tested his ideas through behavior, only to collect more facts, etc., and thus repeat the process over and over. Suffice it to say that the contemporary view no longer sees "sensation" simply as the immediate effect of the environment on the organism nor "perception" simply as the elaboration of these sensations. Experience is now viewed as a give-and-take affair in which the person's motives, past experiences, and learned habits have equal weight with the situation in determining the meaning of events.

Thus, religious experiences do not just happen *to* persons. Persons seek them out, expect them to occur, welcome them when they come, and interpret them through categories supplied by their past experience. Pahnke's Good Friday worshippers, to whom Clark refers, did not interpret the experience without guidance. They were given Stace's categories of mystical experience on which to rate the event. They were provided a structure. More often than not, a worshipper knows what to expect, and although the ecstasy of it may come as a surprise, he yet can talk about it in terms which are readily understood. Clark implicitly agrees with this position when he suggests that the taking of LSD can have most religious meaning when both the guide and the subject intend it to be so.

These are examples of how religious constructs function in religious experience. Like all other constructs utilized by active minds in adapting to their environments, they interpenetrate on the events and give them meaning.

Very few psychologists would take issue with this point of view, although they might disagree concerning the extent to which a person's prior expectations either blind him from or open him up to experience. This is the continuing dialogue between simply reporting events, as in pure phenomenology and behaviorism, and deductive hypothesis testing, as in controlled experimentation. There may be a need to be open to novel, unexpected events or "serendipity" as Skinner terms it, but no psychologist would affirm the possibility of observing "facts" without some assumptions or theories. As Helson asserted, we cannot "operate without a theory" (1964, p. 2). To a greater or lesser extent, this is always true, even in religious experience.

In Clark's discussion of mystical experiences reported in both his and Pahnke's experiments, these issues are confused. He seems to imply the interpretations arise out of the experience, but one wonders what the participants would have said had they not been provided a convenient checklist based on Stace's categories of mysticism. It would seem as if the meaning of the events did not arise spontaneously from the event itself but that it was provided by a tradition whose constructs were provided.

Interestingly enough, there is some contradictory evidence, as reported by Havens (1964). Several researchers uniformly found that the explicit anticipation of a religious experience did not correlate significantly with their occurrence under drugs. Perhaps the meaning is supplied less by one's conscious *set* and more by the deeply engrained thought forms of the culturally supplied religion which one brings unconsciously to the event. This may explain why Leary and Clark (1963) found that although less than ten per cent of their sample were churchgoers or believers, yet religious reports of the experience occurred in over half the subjects. Nevertheless, at least one author would agree with Clark and insist that experience in itself is "implicitly meaningful" (Gendlin, 1962). In a consideration of the psychotherapeutic process, he encourages the therapist to assist persons in becoming sensitive to what they are experiencing at a preverbal, feeling level. These experiences are implicitly meaningful and can, in fact, guide conceptualization at a later time. Thus, persons are encouraged to trust their feelings and let them speak for themselves. Nevertheless, in spite of proposing that experience per se is inherently meaningful, Gendlin does suggest that a given experience may contain very many different conceptual meanings. This last idea indicates some acknowledgment of the viewpoint offered earlier in this essay, namely that the set of religious constructs one brings to an experience predetermines its meaning. Havens (1964) expresses it thusly, "My own limited observation: . . . suggests that the *deepest* and *most personally significant* spiritual encounters came to those who were prepared for them" (p. 224). He quoted one author as explicitly stating the experience *confirmed* the ideas about religion and life he had held long before.*

THE DEVELOPMENT AND USES
OF RELIGIOUS CONSTRUCTS

Turning next to a more detailed discussion of religious constructs, two aspects need to be considered: their dynamic meaning and their development.

Concerning the development of religious constructs, Elkind (1970) proposes a model wherein the child's evolving cognitive

*These considerations have their parallel in the historic reason-revelation dichotomy. This dimension of the discussion cannot be ignored, even though psychologists may choose to bypass it with an emphasis on functionalism. There may be operating an implicit negative metaphysics of the Watsonian variety when psychologists claim they have only the tools to study human experience and therefore cannot make statements about variables apart from it. Carl Jung probably illustrated this position in saying "I do not believe in God, I know him." This essay will try to remain sensitive to this issue in spite of the fact that it will primarily concern itself with the experience of religion from the viewpoint of human behavior.

needs (cf. Piaget) are met via four major elements in institutional religion. The early search for permanence, or conservation, is met through faith in God who does not change and who gives eternal life to believers. The search for symbols, or representation, is met through Scriptures which stand for the divine and represent Him. The search for cause-and-effect understanding, or relationships, is met in worship wherein the youth relates himself to God. During adolescence the search for theories, or comprehension, is met in the history and sagas (theology) of faith which integrates youth's understanding of God in His various aspects.

Each of these needs, while begun at definite times during childhood, persists throughout life. The person's perception of God, scripture, worship, and theology becomes progressively more elaborate and comes to comprise a system and/or way of life. In each case, the person brings to his inevitable conflicts with social and physical reality the ready-made solutions of his religious heritage which he subsequently uniquely applies. As Allport (1955) has said, real law is unique. This would mean that each person's concept of God, Scripture, worship, and theology is, in an ultimate sense, his alone. The use of the same words to apply to two people (e.g. they believe the scripture is the word of God) is only for convenience. The real unity is each person's belief as it relates to the organization of elements in his own personality. No two beliefs are really the same. Each person's faith is uniquely his own. Similarities are probably more apparent than real. Religious concepts serve individual needs and are uniquely adapted to each person's life.

In reconsidering the Clark-type experiment of drug-induced religious experiences, one might wonder how Clark would accord his categories with Elkind's developmental ideas. To what adaptive problem and to which cognitive need does the experience speak? The age of the subjects would certainly indicate an ability to think abstractly or use formal operations, in Piaget's terms. Certainly mystery is a part of experience from an early time in life. One suspects, however, that it was not just mystery that Clark's subjects were explaining with their self reports but, in addition, answers to their search for meaning and self realization. At least one of the subjects, who was previously agnostic, entered seminary after the experience. This attests to the functional, adaptive quality suggested above.

Elkind easily moves the discussion into the second aspect, namely the dynamic meaning of religious constructs. In general, it could be reaffirmed that their meaning is largely utilitarian. That is, they serve a function in the life of the individual. It has already been stated that they function as all other perceptions in that they help make meaning out of experience. But the impetus to make meaning is itself grounded in a more pervasive motivational system. This system has been variously referred to adjustment, adaptation and/or self-realization.

Elkind's (1970) emphasis is on the meeting of adaptive needs. Erikson's (1958) treatment of Luther also emphasizes personal adaptation. Freud's (1964) discussion of projection in religion is illustrative of the adjustment use of constructs. Pfister's (1948) interpretation of dogma as defensive rationalization is also in this tradition. Carl Jung's (1963B) theorizing, which suggests that people "make" their god, exemplifies the self-realization position. Also, Tillich (1952) suggested that religious symbols serve this function of providing meaning for the self's pilgrimage. It is sufficient to say that there has been wide agreement since the time of William James that people use their God, and the words they use to describe Him have dynamic, idiosyncratic meaning for their lives.

One can affirm this functional understanding of religion without at the same time falling into a pure subjectivism or reductionism. Concerning subjectivism, Jung noted the almost universal religious concern among persons who have sought to know themselves. There is a "collective" dimension to religion which is interindividual and not subjective. Concerning reduction-ism, it can be reiterated that to suggest religion is functional does not say its constructs have no additional meaning nor does it automatically reduce faith to body chemistry. Function can be conceived in terms of levels of organization and interrelated systems. Religion can be understood as functional at the level of bringing meaning and integration into life. Boisen (1936), in writing of the function of religion in mental illness, demonstrates this viewpoint. He describes the ways in which persons face the dilemma of meaninglessness and pointlessness through experiencing God's judgment and superlative power. It is a function which need not be reduced, as some writers have done.

There is a final dimension of utility to which Clark refers in his third lecture. He discusses the "fruits" or results of religious experience. To perceive religious experience and constructs as serving the functions of adaptation and/or self-realization is probably secondary to the issue of how religion functions to motivate subsequent or future behavior. One of the ongoing concerns of theologicans has been the supposed lack of ethical outcomes eventuating from religious experience. Seemingly, much religious experience has served solely to resolve preexisting adaptation or self-realization problems. Thus, those groups that have emphasized "experience" have been suspect. In fact, many have agreed with William James in his assertion that religious experience should be judged by its *fruits* rather than its *roots* (or origins). Haven's (1964, pp. 220-221) puts it thusly in discussing the validity of drug induced religious experiences:

> . . . any new knowledge acquired under the psychedelic drugs must be subjected to the tests of *reason* and *subsequent experience*. . . . Do the insights lead toward the deepening of human relations, toward perceiving the world more accurately, toward freedom from ego-centeredness? Do they jibe with those already-affirmed values around which one disposes one's life?

Clark's reports of the changes that occurred in the life of the criminal are noteworthy, as are his comments regarding the good citizenship displayed by many Pentecostals in South America. Further evidence (Whitaker, 1971) tends to support these impressions and to suggest that these charismatic movements are providing leadership in many social-action movements in Latin America. Not only are they becoming responsible citizens but they are challenging social structures and establishing services for the inadequate and poor. Manuel deNelo, one of the better known Pentecostal evangelists, is widely feared by politicians because of the votes that he controls. He regularly speaks out for social justice. Finally, in the United States, the Pentecostals have led the way in working with drug addicts and problem youth. Their rate of cure, in such programs as Teen Challenge, is widely acknowledged to equal, if not surpass, the rate of cure in governmental services. Further, the growing emergence of Christian communes, such as Our Father's Family in Pasadena, California, is evidence of a successful effort to reach confused youth. Here, too, the level of personal integration and purpose seems to equal, if not surpass, the results of many other social-welfare agencies.

Clark's somewhat simplistic assumption that morals flow from experience was noted earlier. This impression may be due more to what he did not say than what he did. However, this issue is a critical one in discussing the ethical fruits of religious experience. The Pentecostals who express their faith in ethical ways would no doubt see themselves as behaving theologically. That is, they would not report an intent just to be good moral citizens but instead would say they were responding in love to God's gift of their salvation. These are theological statements which make meaning of their religious experiences and guide their behavior. Their behavior is not simply the result of a mysterious conscious-ness, expanding event, per se. As Harman (1968, pp. 199-200) states

> ...the experiences sometimes result in observable changes...in personality and behavior patterns... when these changes take place, they are functions of a whole constellation of factors — expectations of the subject and therapist, the subject's trust in the therapist and himself, the context within which the drug is taken, the general cultural milieu, the idiosyncratic nature of the subject — and not a specific drug reaction... one over-simplifies by assuming that the particular part of this spectrum that one may have encountered represents "what LSD does.

If one does not presume the structuring import of religious constructs on these experiences, one has no way to judge the behaviors which result from them save under the umbrella of that which is socially acceptable. I do not think Clark meant this but it is implied.

O. Hobart Mowrer (1961) illustrates this error. He, too, calls for a judgment of religious experience on the basis of ethical results. Yet his basis for evaluating these ethics lies in conformity to cultural expectations and the Golden Rule. Conscience, for Mowrer, functions to convict a man of violating the rules of the society in which he lives. It does not, as in theological ethics, convince him that his relationship and response to God has been disrupted. Mowrer's position runs the danger of naively assuming that the validity of the fruits of religious experience can be judged by the degree of cultural conformity. This has led in some cases to a "work's righteousness" position in which the judgmental encounter nature of Christian relgious experience has been completely forgotten. Mowrer himself has become an ethical humanist.

Suffice it to say that the nature of theological ethics is grounded in the experience of encounter within the religious experience. The behavior of the religious person, so conceived, is a response to this encounter. Good deeds are judged, in the case of Christian ethics, by the loving nature of the God who revealed himself in Jesus Christ and who called the believer (or experiencer) into fellowhip and service. This theological conception, brought to the experience, provides the norm for ethics and guides behavior. It is by no means a simple result of experience itself, as Clark infers, nor is its norm a matter of cultural conformity.

Two final comments are in order. The first has to do with the place of the contrived inducement of religious experiences while the second is concerned with the need for reexperiencing among this generation.

INDUCED RELIGIOUS EXPERIENCE

In his discussion of conversion, Clark suggested it was good that conversion was no longer required and that coercion was a poor climate for religious experience. I disagree on both points because I think Clark himself believes neither of them. On the one hand, it is highly questionable whether religion can have any meaning apart from experience. The mechanical passing down of religious constructs may be a sterile exercise unless it is accompanied by an experiential event whose meaning is illumined by them. On the other hand, such experiences may never occur where they are not expected and elicited through situational inducement. Coercion, herein defined as planning for and controlling a situation, may be the *only* way religious experiences can happen.

Thus, I do not qualitatively distinguish a planned worship service from Pahnke's drug-induced Good Friday experiment. Both are coercion, defined as artificial inducement. In fact, it could be said that all worship is contrived. Pruyser (1968) notes that sitting still, kneeling, bowing the head, adorning the altar, reading responsively, preaching in sober voice, playing the organ prelude — all are contrived means to induce religious experience. The more remarkable measures, such as fasting, going alone to the desert, praying through the night, and pleading for decision, are simply differences in degree, not kind, from the commonplace inducements. Pruyser (1968, p. 22) continues by stating:

> Through demanding physical exercises, dietary experiments, regulated breathing, posturing, and dancing, through the ingestion of toxins, through sleep deprivation and exposure to noxious stimuli, through concentrated medications or rhythmic shouting and handclapping, devout people all over the world have tried to change their ordinary perceptual acumen to that state of brightness of which can be said 'Behold, I make all things new.'

Thus, there is warrant for agreeing with Clark that just because the "triggers" of an experience are contrived, trivial, or artificial does not invalidate the event. As has been said, all efforts at ritual or in declaring certain articles, places, and action sacred are contrivances. Planning circumstances which enhance the likelihood of a religious experience occurring is the norm, not the exception, as some have thought.

The radical difference between drug-induced experience and other religious practices may be that the drugs, e.g. LSD and psilocybin, have not been set aside by a religious community as a sacred article or act for use in the inducement of religious experience. (The exception to this is, of course, the Peyote Indians). The larger community (i.e. the nation) has declared these drugs harmful to society. For religionists, cultural proscription alone never has been, nor should it be, the sole basis for assessing the value of a given practice. Nevertheless, there is a continuing debate over the ultimate benefit or possible harm of such drugs. For example, Havens (1964) reports two contrasting emphases in research with these hallucenogenic drugs. Biochemical psychiatric research seems to emphasize their psychotomimetic (psychotic symptom producing) qualities, while psychotherapeutic research considers them to be revelatory and thus beneficial to mental health. At this moment, society seems to have elected to affirm the former and deny the latter. Therefore, there is a question as to whether religionists can continue to utilize so controversial a "trigger." Are there not more benign means of achieving the same ends? Gunther (1970), among others, feels there is, as indicated by the subtitle of his recent book *What to Do Til the Messiah Comes.* This subtitle is "Non-drug ways to grow flow on."

THE NEW DEMAND FOR EXPERIENCE IN RELIGION

This leads to the second issue concerning the continuing importance of experience in the religious life of each new generation. Numerous writers have noted the need for each generation to reexperience the meaning underlying the concepts of religion. Tillich (1952) suggested that each age needed to formulate its own myths out of its unique existential questions. Henry Murray (1960) spoke of the current need for vital or living myths to replace the senescence of traditional religion. Hope, according to Bakan (1966), lies in the continual "breaking through" of the unmanifest into life. Death, on the other hand, lies in passive acceptance of the rigid structure handed down by tradition. Barron (1963) sees the expansion of consciousness, so essential to creativity, as a "spiritual" task to be engaged in with utter seriousness. Jung (1933) in his *Modern Man in Search of a Soul* is probably the most lucid description of the need for enlivening the old with new experience. In fact, religion, for Jung, is a willingness to reflect on oneself and be faithful in acknowledging the depths of one's experience. There is, thus, much agreement with Clark's call for making oneself vulnerable to new experience in order to break through the tendency to be overly cognitive, rationalize faith or hang on to sterile ideas.

I affirm the above emphasis for, as has been said, God cannot be borrowed. Jung (1963, p. 85) stated "Nietzsche was no atheist, but his God was dead." He continued (p. 89):

> (I speak to . . .) those many people for whom the light has gone out, the mystery has faded, and God is dead. For most of them there is no going back, and one does not know either whether going back is

always the better way. To gain an understanding of religious matters, probably all that is left us today is the psychological approach . . . to try to melt them down again and pour them into molds of immediate experience.

There is a continuing need for new religious experiences in each generation. In fact, I would be so bold as to say experience, not dogma, is the seed of faith. Religion will not last without it. Certainly many in this generation are calling for new experience.

The critical question, as Havens (1968, p. 118) notes in a chapter on "new religion," is whether ". . . we are searching for genuinely new myths and theological formulations, or (whether we are) seeking primarily the revitalization of old myths and doctrines."

There are those who affirm each viewpoint. The weight of this essay would seem to be on the side of revitalizing the old myths. Since it has been asserted that religious constructs are brought to experience, it would seem as if tradition is handed down through making meaning of new events. Rubenstein (1968), a student of Judaism and psychoanalysis, agrees with this position and suggests that the old symbols can be brought to life. He recognizes the danger of what he terms "bad faith" — i.e. people avoiding reexperiencing the meaning of their religious traditions and using the symbols to make themselves feel comfortable. Yet he sees the ultimate significance of both life experiences and the faith answers of traditional religion and feels they are more valuable than newly created symbols.

The question remains as to whether it is possible for modern man to be true to his creative potentialities yet sense the validity of those religious ideas handed down to him from his elders? However, this is a risk which must be taken, because experience is the essence of a man's perception and thought. Words are dead without it. Clark is to be commended for his emphasis on the importance of experience.

In summary, this essay has been an attempt to respond to the Finch Symposium Lectures of W. H. Clark printed earlier in this volume. Religious experience was herein interpreted as psychologically similar to all other experience, in spite of its special object and constructs. Thus Clark's concern for uniqueness was reevaluated. A discussion of the importance of religious constructs in perception was followed by sections on their development and function. Finally, the critical issues of the validity of induced experience and the necessity of reexperiencing were considered. The intent of the essay was to reaffirm Clark's emphasis on the primacy of experience while reconsidering his exclusive emphasis on religious uniqueness and his inclusive viewpoint that ethics flow unilaterally from the experience itself.

REFERENCES

Allport, G.: Becoming: basic considerations for a psychology of personality. New Haven, Connecticut, Yale University Press, 1955.

Bakan, D.: The duality of human existence: An essay on psychology and religion. Chicago, Rand-McNally, 1966.

Barron, F.: Creativity and psychological health. Princeton, New Jersey, D. Van Nostrand, 1963.

Boisen, A.: The exploration of the inner world. New York, Harper and Row, 1936.

Bruner, J. S., Goodnow, J. J., and Austin, G. A.: A study of thinking. New York, Wiley, 1956.

Dittes, J.: Psychology of religion. In G. Lindzey and E. Aronson. The handbook of social psychology, (2nd ed.). Reading, Massachusetts, Addison-Wesley, 1969, 602-659.

Elkind, D.: The origins of religion in the child. Review of Religious Research, 1970, 12 (1), 35-42.

Erikson, E.: Young man Luther. New York, Norton, 1958.

Freud, S.: The Future of an illusion. Garden City, New York, Double-day Anchor, 1964.

Gendlin, E.: Experiencing and the creation of meaning. New York, Free Press, 1962.

Gunther, B.: What to do 'til the Messiah comes. New York, Collier Books, 1970.

Harman, W. W.: The psychedelic experience. In H.A. Otto and J. Mann Ways of growth. New York, Grossman Publishers, 1968, 199-212.

Havens, J.: Memo on the religious implications of the consciousness-changing drugs. Journal for the Scientific Study of Religion, 1964, III, 216-226.

Havens, J. (Ed.): Psychology and religion: A contemporary dialogue. Princeton, New Jersey, Van Nostrand, Insight Book, 1968.

Helson, H.: Adaptation level theory. New York, Harper and Row, 1964.

James, W.: The varieties of religious experience. New York, New American Library, 1961.

Jung, C.: Modern man in search of a soul. New York, Harcourt, Brace and World, 1933.

Jung, C.: Psychological commentary on the Tibetian book of the dead. In C. Jung Psychology and religion: west and east. New York, Pantheon Books, 1963a, 475-508.

Jung, C.: Psychology and religion. In C. Jung Psychology and religion: west and east. New York, Pantheon Books, 1963b, 3-106.

Kelly, G. A.: The psychology of personal constructs, 2 Vol. New York, Norton, 1955.

Leary, T. and Clark, W. H.: Religious implications of the consciousness expanding drugs. Religious Education, 1963, May-June, 251-256.

Mowrer, O. H.: The crisis in psychiatry and religion. Princeton, New Jersey, Van Nostrand, Insight Book, 1962.

Murray, H.: Myths and myth making. New York, G. Braziller, 1960.

Pfister, O.: Christianity and fear. London, George Allen and Unwin, 1948.

Pruyser, P.: A dynamic psychology of religion. New York, Harper and Row, 1968.

Rubenstein, R.: The symbols of Judaism and religious existentialism. The Reconstructionist. 1959, 14, 13-19.

Tillich, P.: Systematic theology (Vol. 1). Chicago, University of Chicago Press, 1951.

Tillich, P.: The courage to be. New Haven, Connecticut, Yale University Press, 1952.

Tillich, P.: The relation of religion and health. In S. Doniger (Ed.) Religion and health. New York, Association Press, 1958.

Whitaker, R. C.: The social concerns of Pentecostals. Paper presented at Conference on Christian Renewal, Methodist Theological School, Kansas City, Missouri, April 1971.

Chapter 6

THE PHENOMENOLOGY OF WORSHIP, CONVERSION AND BROTHERHOOD
An Anthropologist's Point of View

A. R. TIPPETT

THE committee organizing this series of lectures considered it appropriate to include among the reactors a social anthropologist with a missionary interest. My role, after a general reaction, is to point out the implication of Dr. Clark's series of lectures for cross-cultural situations, such as those met on the mission-field, with respect to conversion and other mystical experiences. Thus, I hope to achieve Clark's own expressed desire, i.e. that the lectures "may be *used*."

As one who is much concerned with the experiential aspect of religion, both in conversion and postconversion phenomena, and particularly with persons coming out of animism into Christianity, perhaps I should first extract from the lectures those features with which I agree, and which I can accept as a common basis for interaction. Following this, I shall record briefly a number of matters about which I have some reservations. Finally I shall react against the logic of his conclusion, which, although in one sense it may aid human relations, nevertheless represents an untenable position for the cross-cultural Christian mission.

I am prepared to accept Dr. Clark's subjective involvement in *participant observation,* because I recognize that certain data can be collected only subjectively. The purely objective observer (if such a person exists) cannot evaluate adequately phenomonological data which he himself has not experienced. I have not participated in chemical ecstasy like the lecturer, but I have participated cross-culturally in mystical experiences that have not

92

been self-induced. Possibly my rejection of the interpretive conclusion is my own subjective bias reacting against the subjective bias of the lecturer.

AGREEMENT

Dr. Clark's lectures render a major service to the study of religion by calling us back to a dimension which for some years now, has been seriously threatened. This appears to be the basic stimulus or motive of his presentation, and because I agree wholeheartedly with this contention, I feel that here we have a basis for discussion. The main points of his thesis, with which I concur may be summarized as follows:

1. I accept the differentiation between the *rational* (interpretive) and *nonrational* (feelings) as the components of religious experience, including the distinction of the irrational from the nonrational.

2. I agree that there needs to be a balance between these two components, which are like the rudder and engine of a ship.

3. Even so, there is a danger of *reductionism* — the reduction of religion to one of the components at the expense of the other. I agree that either one without the other is dangerous.

4. I am prepared to agree with Dr. Clark's criticism that religious life today is largely reductionism towards the rational dimension or of one of its components — chemical elements, father image, moral rules, need for protection, or the philosophical search for meaning — and that too often the nonrational — feeling, sense of awe, idea of the Holy, mysticism or religious ecstasy — is rejected. The emphasis on the rational at the expense of the nonrational has led to the Church's stress on *organization* rather than on *encounter with God;* institutions destroy themselves by dogma; programs and sermons become onesided; what passes for religion is cold for the want of it. Allowing for the weakness of all such generalizations, I think that this is "generally true."

5. If we accept that generalization, I agree that there is some justification for the lecturer's contention that awareness of this imbalance lies behind the vigor of mystical and drug experimentation as seen in the modern counterculture and also in Pente-

costalism and other movements. Anthropologically I tend to see these movements as a group striving to meet unsatisfied needs. Therefore, whatever we may think of the means employed, I am prepared to accept the basic motivation as natural.

6. The mystical experience of religion is not to be regarded as either an escape or an indulgence. However the experience requires follow-up and discipline to "make it stick." This is agreed.

7. Dr. Clark contends that purely rational religion cannot produce the fullest effects of personal integration, love, joy, and widening sensitivity; that this experience requires experiment, readiness to take risks, the vulnerability of self-exposure to communal discipline, to pentecostalism and/or therapeutic techniques. He claims that the really significant changes (conversion, new life and its new meaning), normally spring from the nonrational experiences, that sudden conversion experiences are more durable, that even glossolaliacs become more stable citizens. This also I find generally true in most cross-cultural situations.

8. One statement, confined to a single sentence in the lectures, but of considerable significance in the cross-cultural situation is that the new life, new meaning, and new sense of values which come with conversion or another mystical experience do not necessarily change the life style. I take this to mean that the convert may still normally continue in his own role and context, manifesting new life and meaning there. I presume this also means that cross-cultural conversion does not have to be culturally foreign.

9. Finally I agree with the lecturer that the mystical experience may be a reflex or negative movement: that is, (a) it may take the form of a counterconversion, or (b) we have also the possibility of some demonic form of mysticism.

I think that I can react with the lecturer on the broad acceptance of the above nine points, which recapitulate much of his argument in his own terminology. Before doing so, however, let me indicate a few reservations.

SOME RESERVATIONS

I appreciated the caution with which the lecturer recommended the use of drugs for inducing chemical ecstasy, and I value his opinion of the data he presented because of his own experimentation. I do not object to a man using himself as a guinea-pig for science's sake. However, as he says, he writes from a Christian point of view, and Christianity being what it is, I have some scruples about the use of chemical ecstasy for religious experience. I am merely expressing reservations at this juncture. The lectures were a brief survey. Not very much data were given at several key points. I see several interpretive possibilities for the data given to us. Chemical ecstasy for inducing more intensified religious sensations could be or become an *escape* or an *indulgence*, which we have agreed is undesirable. (In point of fact, the number of persons for whom it has become just this is alarming.) Or, on the other hand, it could become something imposed by a third party. The possibilities of manipulating the religious experiences of other people are numerous and frightening. This raises all kinds of ethical and theological problems. Deepening one's own experience is one thing, manipulating conversion is another thing altogether. Indeed I would object to calling this conversion at all, conversion being to me a voluntary act, not a chemical control of the will.

Or again, a *self-induced* religious experience (even if medically administered) creates a kind of situation remarkably similar to a number of well-known cross-cultural animistic performances in the area of self-induced spirit possession. Here we run into an awful tangle of values. If self-induced chemical ecstasy for religious experience is justifiable in the West, does the same apply in cross-cultural or primitive situations, where it will certainly be interpreted in terms of spirit possession? The possibilities of abuse and difficulties of control are many. Should a chemical experiment on an individual be approved or disapproved on its own merits, or on a basis of its social effects? How can we ensure that the chemical effects of the drug will be desirable and not precipitate a counterconversion or some demonic form of mysticism — a possibility we have accepted?

Or again, I have known nominally Christian American Indians to indulge in peyote behind their pastor's back. In this act, for shamanistic (healing) purposes, they have intellectually placed Christ in the same category as the Indian holy people; but for the healing and mystical experience they have turned in prayer and adoration to Pioniyo, the peyote spirit — who to them at this point is God. Christianity being what it is, this is manifestly inconsistent. I do not deny that the peyote drug intensifies sensations and deepens religious perceptions, but they are perceptions of God in terms of Pioniyo, not of Christ. It seems, therefore, that the drug does not *cause* the mystical experience, but rather stimulates or intensifies something that is already there — maybe an element of faith, or a fear, or a desire.

I reacted against the lecturer's claim of "lasting conversions" that followed the "use of LSD-type drugs," because under the drug the conscious act of will in conversion would be defective. Later, pressed by a question, he likened the experiment to a developer drawing out what was already on the film, and I was more in agreement. Even so, I am still not quite sure what the evidence cited in the lectures actually proves. Even Dr. Clark's own quantitative drug experiments do not quite satisfy me. Of course, I realize that time did not permit his presentation of all the data and argument, and I do not doubt that the participants had an intensified non-rational experience which they interpreted as religious. Even so, I am curious to know what criteria he used to measure 76 per cent as "experiencing the Holy" and 78 per cent as experiencing "psychological rebirth" (seeing that these terms would not mean the same thing to any two persons) and differentiate these experiences from a physiological drug effect, like a soothing cough syrup on a sore throat or a deep-heat liniment on a bruised body, either of which is a pleasing sensation. I am an anthropologist, not a psychologist, and I am not aware just what precise connotation "psychological rebirth" may have to the speaker beyond some kind of rejuvenation. However the term suggests to me a whole realm of experience in some forms of animism where the religious structures are supplied with new novitiates from time to time by processes of psychological rebirth. These are specific performances, total community festivals, in which persons chosen to become consorts of the god or fetish are separated from the living by death and ceremonially reborn as part of the public presentation. Several forms of possession and mysticism are associated with these resurrection cults.* In many

---

*The reader may find a fine description of one in Tidani's article "Rituels" in *Le Monde Noir,* special number of Presence Africane, 1950.

of these cults, drugs are used to produce the effects and to convince the novitiates of the genuineness of the rebirth. Here again, we have the intensifying of feelings already there in the mind. The drug is more the stimulant than the cause. I do not doubt the reality of the nonrational experience nor that it was religious, but if it was an "experience of the Holy," I venture to suggest that it was an intensification only of the "idea of the Holy" that was already in the mind of the subject before the drug was administered.

If Dr. Clark was depending on the third lecture (on the effects of the experience) to validate his previous examples, then we must admit (as I believe he does) that the ethical outworkings of, say, peace, brotherhood, and unity are not confined alone to Christian experiences. Hindu and Christian ethics may look alike in their social outworkings, although their motivation, religious convictions, and ultimate values are quite different. On the other hand, there is adequate documentation to indicate that the mystical experiences of the pre-Christian Fijian led to very different effects, which reinforced the ethnic entity by a system of war, cannibalism, widow-strangling, and human sacrifice, all of which were tied to religious values. The human "virtues," which built up the merit that assured the Fijian of prosperity in the life beyond, were in terms of war, death, and destruction of enemies, not in peace and brotherhood and new life. The priests who activated the group in this direction did so by self-induced mystical states of possession, and by drumming and communal dancing which transmitted a mystical experience. So this is another reminder that mysticism may be demonic, and in such cases, the effects may be the opposite of feelings of peace and brotherhood.

As to the Pahnke experiment, I react very strongly to this. I fully recognize that my reaction is personal: that is, it is my own self reacting. I do not react because the researcher invaded the inner lives of the theological students, for I presume they were party to the experiment. I react against the very idea of using a chemically controlled drug experiment for attempted measuring of mystical experiences in a Good Friday service. It offends me. At this point I find myself unable to continue "objectively" as an anthropologist. Momentarily I am a religious mystic, who finds the

locus of his mystical experience – his "means of grace" –
desecrated by a profane experiment, which I deeply resent. No
doubt I feel this way because the experiment threatens my own
personal ideas of the prerogatives of the religious person.
Something is being manipulated, a sacred moment is being
explored by a secular individual, whose very attitude shows he
cannot share it, because an investigation is not an act of devotional
participation, requiring the whole self.

It requires a conscious effort for me to break away and be an
anthropologist again. Even then the thing troubles me for
scientific reasons. The experiment seems to measure no more than
that a certain drug has certain physiological effects, which may be
interpreted as religious if the subjects are already religious. The
apparent presupposition that such a control experiment permits
one to measure spirituality is by no means proved. Furthermore, it
seems to assume that there is some way of controlling the spiritual
variables in a good Friday service. I cannot conceptualize any
scientifically valid means of doing this. From the limited data in
the lectures, I am led to imagine that the theological students are
taken as a representative group of such persons. But their readiness
to be involved in such an experiment suggests they all stood much
nearer the rational pole than the nonrational, and this would in
itself tend to reflect their intellectual speculations and scientific
expectations. I am not opposed to control experiments as a
research method, but many researchers use it where variables
cannot even be identified, let alone controlled. The whole thing
lacks credibility.

THE NATURE OF CONVERSION

I also have some difficulty with the lecturer's model or
definition of conversion as a change from nonfaith to faith. This
seems to me to be a partial view of the process, which does not
allow for the whole person, the whole context, or the whole
sequence. Conversion is not an initial experience of faith, but a
change from *that-faith* to *this-faith*. Moving from *not-having* to
having is quite a different thing from moving from *having-this* to
having-that. In one sense we are dealing more with a *redirection* of

faith. New knowledge or experience may lead us to reformulate or redirect our faith, but there never is a state of nonfaith. Sometimes we speak figuratively of the "void in life," either for an individual or multiindividual community, meaning a state of unsatisfied felt-needs. We may speak of a "desire for faith" or a "search for faith." However, the very awareness of this "void," and "desire" or the "search" are themselves expressions of faith, not of nonfaith: the conviction that somewhere out in front there is a more adequate faith-formulation or more adequate frame of reference for one's life operations. Even the agnostic scientist is at base a man of faith. He has faith that the universe operates on the basis of specific laws or regularities. He has faith that these laws are discoverable — that they can be applied for the betterment of man, and faith that he himself can do something about that discovery and/or application. When a scientist makes a new discovery and sees its potential (so that he can act upon it as an innovator), that is not something new put where there was nothing at all before, but rather an attitudinal recombination of elements and relationships (an interpretation of cultural change developed first by Barnett, 1953).

Therefore I react against the lecturer's view of conversion as a process described as a "change of attitude *toward* a faith orientation," or "a change *from a state of general religious unbelief* and disintegration to one of positive integration and effectiveness" (underlining mine). To me this means conversion is only for neurotics. The case cited in the lecture was Saul of Tarsus, converted from a negative attitude to Christianity to a positive one, from an attitude of rejection to one of acceptance. This does not allow for Saul's earlier attitude being an effect, not a cause. He had a positive Judaistic faith. This was not a state of nonbelief. His was not a disintegrated personality. The claim of Christ was being measured against his positive Jewish messianic-hope criteria. The conversion experience introduced a new set of data and demanded a recombination of elements and relationships, which signified a conscious decision which transported him, not from nonfaith to faith, but from a polarized Jewish faith to a Christian faith. This process can be schematized after the model of Barnett's recombination thesis as shown in Figure 1.

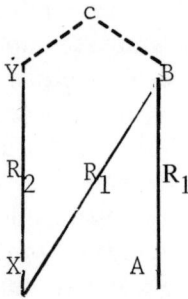

Figure 1. (X) Saul of Tarsus defending (R_2) Jewish religion (Y). (A) Converts preaching (R_1) the Gospel (B). Saul's new experience is X R_1 B, which has him preaching the Gospel instead of defending the Jewish faith. The common factor (c) is the Messianic Hope, which relates both to the Jewish religion and the Christian Gospel.

Somewhere there must come a point (or period) of time when the convert (either individual or multiindividual group) rejects the old faith-formulation and accepts the new one, the point of innovation, when the conceptualized recombination is acted upon. In Western Christianity, this may be manifestly recorded before the fellowship group by an old-fashioned altar-call response, an act of baptism or confirmation, a public testimony, or in many other ways. This ocular or audible demonstration is both an act of rejection and of acceptance, the passage from an old faith-orientation to a new one. The view that it is from nonfaith to faith is partial and ethnocentric, in my opinion.

The idea of passing from nonfaith to faith creates the impression of the transport from spiritual poverty to wealth, a completely "one-way deal." It fails to see the significance of surrendered values and the cost of separation from something that is itself quite positive. Yet that act of separation is important. We Westerners tend to see baptism as an act of incorporation into the fellowship (which it is) but often overlook that its symbolism is supposed to indicate the death of the old man in us. It is as much an act of separation from the old life. A Hindu, converted to Christianity, will see his baptism very much as an act of separation, with very serious social and kinship consequences, for which reason many Indian converts delay their baptism until the whole family group is ready to be baptized together. Anthropologically, this lines up with van Gennep's theory of the *rites of passage* in which he discussed the periods of status change in life — the ceremonial process of the passage from youth to manhood, for example. He saw all these processes of status change as beginning with a *rite of separation* and concluding with a *rite of incorporation* (Van Gennep, 1909).

In dealing with the psychological processes of conversion in cross-cultural situations, as for example in a missionary program in a communally-structured animist society, it is of basic importance for the evangelist (missionary or national) to recognize that the convert (individual or group) is not just moving from nonfaith to faith. He has first to cut himself off from an old, pre-Christian, but nevertheless positive faith; and to demonstrate this in an ocular manner in forms socially meaningful to his fellow-countrymen. This may be by burning his fetishes, burying his mana-charged bones or skulls, throwing his sacred paraphernalia into the sea or river, eating his taboo totemic food, destroying the ancestral grove, or some such visible demonstration. Without this, his fellow countrymen regard the conversion as insincere and likely to be impermanent.*

Where the Christian advocate (missionary or national evangelist) assumes that the process of conversion is merely a passage from a state of nonfaith to faith, he tends to bring about a foreign or westernized conditioning to the resultant Christian congregation, and this can be quite disruptive socially. On the other hand, if he recognizes that something very positive is being surrendered and allows the converts (who are the real innovators) to express themselves through a meaningful act of separation, he tends to retain much more indigenity in his new congregation.

At this point, I would like to recall a point on which we originally agreed; namely, that although conversion will bring new life, new values, and new meaning, this does not necessarily mean a change of life style. One would hope that converts in cross-cultural situations would continue with their daily life, social responsibilities, crafts, musical forms, and their own rather than a foreign language. The new experience has to be worked out as an indigenous thing. Therefore an indigenously conceptualized act of separation from the old faith must begin the act of incorporation into the new. The symbolism has to be meaningful within the mores of the society concerned. In many years of studying

---

*For a more detailed assembly of data and analysis of these procedures see Tippett (1967), Religious Group Conversion in Non-Western Society.

missionary situations anthropologically, I have found that when conversions have come in terms of a philosophical presupposition that the animist target group was to be converted from nonfaith to faith, the result is a foreign type of church, dependent on external supports and authority. On the other hand, where the evangelists have recognized that the process is from one positive faith to another, they have seen their advocacy of the new way in terms of a power encounter in which the convert has to wrestle with spiritual forces and thus have presented their message whole as both an act of rejection and an act of acceptance (not merely an acceptance alone), and some vital indigenous churches have emerged.

If the reader should feel that I have made a song about this point, I would remind him that it is just at this very point that the mission fields of the last century and a half have produced foreign and indigenous churches standing over against each other in contrast. It shows how a theoretical difference, when allowed to determine evangelical attitudes and practice, can have serious consequences for those who follow.

If it should also be felt that I have neglected the disintegrated character of society today and the restorative or therapeutic need of conversion in our time, let me offer the following rejoinder. I see the counterculture in our own society in much the same way, although its members are passing through a transition phase in their faith. For many, the act of separation lies behind them. Many are currently reformulating their faith. This is conditioned by environment, political events, hopes, and fears. Some look forward to something new to be incorporated into in the future, but for many they already are incorporated into a real fraternity, a discrete ethnic group with its own mores, values, and faith. Those who as yet have not reformulated their faith (which does not mean they have no faith; it means they are struggling with adjustments within its composition) we may speak (often van Gennep again) of this as the experience of the *rites of transition,* which vary in duration but come between those of separation and incorporation. To project ourselves again into the mission-field situation, we frequently find that the operation of medical and welfare workers have the effect of undermining the reputation of the local shaman, on whom the people have depended hitherto for healing. This loss of tribal confidence in the tribal practitioner and his cures and the awareness of benefits of the nearby missionary clinic frequently precede the conversion of large groups to Christianity. There is a period of faith-conflict. I am not certain that disintegration is the right word, because the people will not tolerate a faith-void, and they have never completely lost control of the situation, and they have never lost faith in the idea of faith. It is a period of recombination of faith elements and relationships, and a matter for multiindividual action. These people will probably become Christian in family or even larger groups. The eventual decision will tend to be a rational rather than a nonrational one, unless some specific mystical experience is shared by the group and brings them to a sudden consensus.

The mention of *consensus* raises a dimension which is not explored in the lectures, but if these are "to be used" with respect to communal societies where conversion is mainly executed by group action, the matter must be discussed. The picture of the conversion experience itself in stages of conflict with sin, surrender to God, and the final state of peace, worked out on the model of Augustine's experience, although not confined to the West, is nevertheless quite Western in this presentation. Augustine here is an individual, pure and simple. He has no context. He is not a person influencing others and being influenced by others. We have a three-panel picture of an individual's mind as an isolate, bodiless in the dark. As an anthropologist, I am disposed to argue with such a picture, even for Western society. I do not believe conversion is ever purely an experience in individual isolation, although each individual must himself be the actor. Conversion is a sociopsychological phenomenon in which the individual gives to and draws from other individuals and groups and activates his individualism within the limits of prescribed patterns. In many societies, the weightage is a clear bias towards the group entity rather than the individual, though in no society is the individual of no significance at all. Many societies safeguard their perpetuity on a basis of consensus. This consensus is reached by multiindividual interaction until all are agreed, then the innovation or change is made by united action with some public symbolic demonstration. Millions of extended families have become Christian in this way. Sometimes it takes longer for decision to be reached, but there can be real mystical excitement when the great day arrives, and the conversion has more abiding solidarity. If the valuable dimensions of these lectures are to be used in such communal societies, a good deal more research needs to be done in the psychology of group conversion.

Perhaps, in an attempt to relate these lectures to religious experience in the missionary world, some mention should be made of the distinction Dr. Clark made between conversion and mysticism. This would be shared on the mission field where two types of mystical experience are met; first, bringing converts out of animism into Christianity (which I have discussed at length) and second, deepening their spiritual lives thereafter. The speaker stressed that conversions needed follow-up in discipline and instruction or there might well be backsliding. This may be mostly at the rational level of religion but regular renewal at the nonrational level leading to revitalization or rededication gives a Christian community a deeper inner life and a more practical outreach. I agree with Clark that mystical experiences are a good thing in religion, that currently the Church tends to push the rational and neglect the nonrational, and for this she is much the poorer. I agree that transcending changes have come into human life through mystical experiences and that these changes have had more permanent and far-reaching effects than intellectual speculations; but this is not to say I think they should be induced by drugs. What the lecturer did not at any place examine was the degree to which the mystical experience is, in point of fact, an act of God. The great and powerful mystical experiences of the Great Awakening of Tonga and Fiji, which turned huge social units from cannibalism to Christianity overnight, although they took place while people were meeting for the regular "means of grace," were quite unexpected, with no psychological build-up, no chemical catalysts, and no controlled experiments for they were total events. If we accept the idea that a mystical experience may be activated by means of drugs, or of psychic, spiritualistic, meditative, or demonic forces, for which evidence can be produced, we have still not actually proved that this is the same kind of thing as happened, presumably by act of God, in the Great Awakening I have just mentioned or in the Christian Endeavour revivals of my own youth. That things appear to be, or look alike, does not actually establish affinity. This may seem to be just a philosophical issue. In point of fact it has profound consequences.

DR. CLARK'S CONCLUSIONS

In terminating the third lecture, Dr. Clark reminded us of the series of national revolutions in modern history and suggested that in this transitory world, only the religions have shown institutional durability. He saw the only hope for the world in "some way to harness the religious consciousness to politics," and the only hope of this he saw on the level of mysticism, for here alone there is unity and brotherhood. This thought had come up in two or three places and in the question periods after the lectures. He had pointed out that the concepts of "being one in Christ" and Nirvana were phenomenologically alike, though far apart in interpretation. Therefore, at the interpretative level, we find disagreement and schism; but our ecumenical hopes lie at the mystical level where we can share. This has a flavor of Toynbee's idea of the need for unity among all who believe in the supernatural as against the man-worshippers (Toynbee, 1956).

Danielou (1967) has also recognized this common element among all the religions, including those of the pure animists, but this classification he has placed at the bottom of the scale. With this I agree. Any unity between the religions on a basis of the lowest common denominator would mean the lowest possible kind of religious unity, and this creates some very serious philosophical obstructions. A unity on a basis of an experience without allowing for *meaning* would be a nonhuman experience, for human beings cannot tolerate phenomena without ascribing meaning to them, and the moment you intellectualize, according to Dr. Clark you create disagreement. Furthermore, then, it would reduce the religious character of the unity to physiological sensation, which is again subhuman. The moment that sensation is registered as a feeling of peace or brotherhood, the non-rational has a rational garment. If the assumption is that peace and brotherhood are universal values, this has to be challenged. There are demonic religions whose mystical experiences do not aspire to peace and brotherhood, and they could not be part of any universal religion without conversion of some kind. At the rational end of the scale, there are some whose materialistic faith denies them the search for communion in mystical experiences.

Any kind of world unity on a basis of religion as the religions now stand is manifestly impossible. Those religions whose norms and values are laid down in sacred literature could not be consistent within themselves in any form of universalism. Those faiths which claim to be universalist should recognize that they are selective; that there are some faiths they could never receive, and there are others who could never retain their integrity if they joined. If man is to be man, he must have the right to worship, ascribe meaning and interpret as he will. If religion is to be a human characteristic, men must be free to disagree about it and religion must provide ways for reconciling men in those disagreements. This is the risk of being human and being humanly religious. There is only one way to resolve this disagreement: namely, by the conversion of the world to one faith. There are Moslems, Buddhists, Hindus, Christians, and Animists in this very city trying to do this very thing. Thus, for example, Christianity, to be itself, as laid down in its Scriptures, is committed to the task of "preaching the gospel to all nations," of "summing up all things in Christ," and of working to that day when He shall be recognized as "King of Kings and Lord of Lords." If it did not work to this end, it would not be Christianity.

I am not saying that men should not work for peace and brotherhood. I believe they certainly should, both for anthropological reasons and because as a Christian, I consider these highly important values. I would also hope that Christians may influence non-Christians in this same direction. Unless we do, I have fears for our survival. I would regard it as our Christian duty to press for a better and more just world with all men seeing each other as brothers. But I do not believe this because it is the sum of the wisdom of the great religious leaders of all religions. That "this is a broad human sympathy and compassion, the fruit of mystical consciousness, *through which alone* man may sense immediately the unity of all things and all creatures, and the brotherhood of man" (italics mine) I do not believe. My personal belief in the brotherhood of man stands on my own personal religion, from which I have learned to know God as my Father, and Christ as the Son, and my own adoption as a son, for the Spirit bears witness with my spirit that I am a son and heir. For this trinitarian belief, for which, as a Christian, I can cite the appropriate Scripture, leads me to see the possibility of adoption for all my brothers. But I can only see the brotherhood of man because I first see the Fatherhood of God. This is an intellectual, a rational position. It is confirmed and stimulated from time to time by my nonrational experiences, but it never came from the sum of the enlightenment of the great mystics of other faiths. This is not to deny a person of another faith the right to such a belief in the brotherhood of man, but to assert that for me it came from the Christian Scriptures, and it has certain theological undergirdings that speak meaningfully only to committed Christians. A Buddhist, a Confucian, and a Christian might agree that all men should be treated as brothers, each for different theological reasons. If they shared a mystical experience, would it itensify the feeling of brotherhood itself or the theological beliefs on which the feeling rested or both? If it were to achieve the goals set out above, it would have to be divested of its theological trimmings, and then on what kind of a base would it stand?

Although Dr. Clark did not deal directly with his subject as it applied to cross-cultural situations, he was seeking a mystical base for a universal experience as a way to peace and brotherhood. I found two problems of approach: two dimensions of investigation that seem to me to call for more consideration before his researches can be considered in any way as universals. Even if one validates a claim for individuals in the sophisticated West, this does not automatically validate claims for other cultural systems. The validity has to be proved in each. In the second place, what may be legitimate for an individualistic Westerner may not be so where an individual is playing his life-role within a tightly structured communal society. Yet any attempt at a universal basis for experience must meet these two conditions.

The problem is not that different societies have different types of personalities. The *distribution* of personality types within a society may be very different and this diversity of distribution may reverse values, so that the normalities of one society become the abnormalities of another. This, I imagine, would mean that chemical ecstasy would produce the opposite effects on the persons and militate against universal values.

If we concede (only for sake of discussion) the point that it is legitimate to experiment with chemical ecstasy in the sophisticated West (but even there we have to insist on strict controls so that it is administered only by qualified practitioners and in controlled doses), are we to assume that this is also practical the wide world over? Even if we confine our thinking to this country, could this be done for the Indians of the Native American Church (the Peyote religion), who interpret their indulgence as a sacrament? As most communal groups who take drugs for cultic purposes are esoteric operations, I do not see any practical way of controlling practitioner or dosage. Therefore I should be disposed to avoid legislation which required double standards. The attempt to justify chemical ecstasy for the Christian by arguing that it is attitudinally similar to prayer and worship, by which means a person seeks communion with God, is no more than an argument by analogy. It does not allow for the fact that prayer, worship, liturgy, the sacraments, and the like stand on scriptural directives — a religious authority which we do not have for chemical ecstasy. Furthermore there is no biological danger from an overdose of the "means of grace." Thus the lecturer is thrown back on the obligation of proving that chemical ecstasy is either a physical need of the body or has some therapeutic value as a religious corrective for neurotics. This cannot be done by analogy.

The advocate of chemical ecstasy is also obligated to show how he intends achieving a moral and not a demonic response, and especially where the subject is known to worship an evil spirit or Satan — for which one does not have to leave the urban area.

One recalls that with another form of ecstasy Paul did not advise the Corinthians to cultivate it, but rather to seek a more excellent way; and John Wesley, who was not unfamiliar with ecstatic experiences layed down spiritual rules for testing enthusiasm and opposed the idea of self-induced ecstasy. In the anthropological taxonomy of ecstatic religious experiences, it is customary for the observer to determine if the experience he is describing is self-induced or "something coming spontaneously from the supernatural," and also whether it is individual or collective. By collective I mean multiindividual group participation. These differentiations in classification have not come into being by accident but are descriptors that have emerged from research. I would therefore suggest that anthropology has something to offer to psychology in this area of research. If this reaction to the lectures can inspire some joint anthropological-psychological cross-cultural explorations, I shall be more than pleased.

Finally, I must express my appreciation of the effort of the committee responsible for this set of lectures and to Dr. Clark for providing us with the basic material with which we were able to interact. I appreciate the manner in which he eliminated the technical psychological terminology to permit reactions from men of other disciplines like myself. I believe I learned something from the very fact of having to react to the lectures. I am convinced that psychology has something to offer to religious experience in cross-cultural situations, but we have a long way to go before we get an adequate recognition of the precise differences between one cultural complex and another and the significance of these differences for the religious multiindividual community.

REFERENCES

Barnett, H. G.: Innovation: Basis of cultural change. New York, McGraw-Hill, 1953.

Danielou, J.: Christianity and the non-Christian religions. Notre Dame, Fides, 1967.

Tidani, A. S.: "Rituels" Le Monde Noire. Special number Presence Africane, 1950.

Tippett, A. R.: "Religious group conversion in non-Western society." Research in Progress Pamphlet, SWM, 1967.

Toynbee, A.: Christianity among the religions of the world. New York, Scribners, 1956.

Van Gennep, A.: Les Rites de Passage. Paris, Nourry, 1909.

Wesley, J.: Sermon on "Enthusiasm." In Fortyfour Sermons. London, Epworth, 1952.

Chapter 7

REJOINDER ON COMMENTARIES

WALTER HOUSTON CLARK

It is always helpful to a writer to have an opportunity to hear what his friends and critics say about his ideas. To be given a chance to comment on the commentaries means, in addition, that he will be pushed to clarify his thoughts as well as to widen his understandings. I have tried to avoid the defensiveness that comes natural to the scholar in such a position.

To summarize broadly the position of my three critics as I understand them: Dr. Malony objected to my exclusiveness in seeing religious experience as unique and essentially mystical; Dr. Daane complained that my picture of it was not sufficiently Christian; and Dr. Tippett felt my hospitality to drugs as a means to mysticism was unscriptural and that I neglected the social element in religion.

Dr. Daane further accused me of being too much the preacher. While I would hesitate to dignify my position as a "theology," as he does, I do not reject his general accusation. Supposedly, the ideal scholar is a kind of cold, calculating machine with a desire to get at the facts and then to lay down conclusions with which no one can quarrel. Though I hope I have not neglected facts, I must confess to a burning desire to get my points across. I want my audience to agree with me, and if Dr. Daane has detected an evangelist beneath the cold exterior of the scholar, I must agree with his perception. I think all scholars, being only human beings, possess a prejudice in favor of their own positions. Hence the note of evangelism.

Though scholars are apt to speak little of the personal sources of their interests, I believe that their publics are entitled to know at least something of these origins insofar as they throw light on their conclusions. Thus it helps us to understand William James'

110

interest in religion to know that his father had experienced a Swedenborgian "vastation" (Allen, 1967, pp. 17-19), that he had experimented himself with nitrous oxide (James, 1958, p. 298), and that he experienced mysticism in nature (cf. Perry, 1954, pp. 266-267, 364). These will help to justify a few personal comments.

My first personal approach to religious experience was through an early stage of moral rearmament. Both my experience and observation of the influence of this movement on the lives of friends and others (The Oxford Group, 1951) led me to a respect for the power of conversion. Then, during my career as a teacher of literature, I became more aware of the dimension of the mystical. Though I am not a mystic, certain literary passages moved me in a strange way. The conviction of the power and the central nature of the mystical consciousness in the religious life grew through my reading of the Bible, Schleiermacher, Carlyle, Emerson, James, Pratt, Otto, and particularly Stace, as well as Huxley, Koestler, and other contemporary nontheological writers.

This conviction was immensely strengthened by participation in the Good Friday experiment (Pahnke, 1964) that demonstrated that the psychedelics tend to release mystical experience. It was supported further by my own self experiments. The psychedelic drugs do not inject anything new into the human mind but simply elicit hitherto unconscious ideas, powers, and sensitivities residing deeply within the individual human psyche. And all the evidence, my own experience included, such as a night of participation in the Indian peyote ceremony, points to the uniqueness in quality of profound religious experience. My own position could not be more succinctly put than it was by William James (Allen, 1967, p. 425) in a letter to Henry W. Rankin: "The mother sea and fountainhead of all religions lie in the mystical experiences of the individual, taking the word mystical in a very wide sense. All theologies and all ecclesiasticisms are secondary growths superimposed . . ."

REJOINDER TO MALONY

It is in the sense of the above quotation from James that I see religion as unique. Certainly the mystical consciousness is unique, for we know that mystics always have trouble in communicating their experiences to other nonmystics. A favorite analogy, often used, is that of the difficulty one would have in communicating the beauties of a sunset to one born blind. The fact that everyone may be born with mystical potentiality does not alter the fact of its uniqueness any more than the fact that many of us go around talking a great deal about religion despite our never having developed the mystical potentiality and perhaps not even knowing that we possess it.

But I do not claim because I believe that the roots of religion are to be found in mystical and ecstatic experiences, it follows that such experiences are all there is to religion. Indeed in its most intense ecstatic form, mysticism constitutes only a small part of religion, for all of its importance. Particularly the unseen roots are not what the ordinary man normally sees as religion and therefore takes it to be. He sees the religious institutions, especially in their concrete churchly forms, along with their theologies, orthodoxies, ethical systems, religious conventions and churchly activities. James would refer to these as "secondary growths."

It is also the enemies of religion who mistake these secondary growths as its essence. It is when this unique source runs dry that the orthodoxies, dogmatisms, and the desire for power in the churches begin to run rampant. To quote James (1961, p. 263) once again,

> ... when a religion has become an orthodoxy, its day of inwardness is over: the spring is dry; the faithful live at second hand exclusively and stone the prophets in their turn ... The basenesses so commonly charged to religion's account are thus, almost all of them, not chargeable at all to religion proper, but rather to religion's wicked practical partner, the spirit of corporate dominion. And the bigotries are most of them in their turn chargeable to religion's wicked intellectual partner, the spirit of dogmatic dominion ...

On the other hand, even religion in touch with its experiential sources is bound to express itself in very large part through its secondary growths. The practical search for social justice, national righteousness, and human compassion is in part the "fruits" by which Jesus has told his followers to distinguish the true prophet from the false. The interpretation and direction of such activities is promoted through theological thinking and ethical codes supported by vigorous religious institutions. In these secondary areas, I would agree with Dr. Malony that religion is not unique and must be studied by conventional intellectual and social scientific methods.

But even in its mystical roots, where religion is unique, it does not follow that we should deny its uniqueness even though it might turn out that we have no ready-made social scientific techniques by which to study it. Yet, as a matter of fact, the mystical consciousness *has* been studied, and with considerable precision, as Pahnke's and other studies have shown. The chief difficulty with mysticism is that its uniqueness is an inner characteristic, and psychologists are notoriously suspicious of subjectivism. But even here there are scientific methods in the form of systematic regularities by which inner state may be studied as Allport set forth in his The Use of Personal Documents in Psychological Science (1942). In those areas where existing methods are inadequate, new ones need to be devised.

With respect to what Malony and also Tippett see as my oversimplified view of social ethics as the product of religious experience, I must acknowledge a certain amount of truth due to the fact that time and space did not allow me an exhaustive consideration of the subject. However, I claimed for mystical experience not that it was the *only* or invariable source of ethics but simply as *one* of its sources, though I wonder, along with Stace (1960), whether it might be found to be their truest source. I do not believe that we have enough information at the present time to know; but it may be significant that the experience of unity reported by the mystics often tends to identify them with all of humanity, all of nature, and all of life. As I already have noted, it was a mystic who wrote the oft-quoted words, "Send not to inquire for whom the bell tolls; it tolls for thee." Yet I would still acknowledge that ecstatic passion unsupported and unguided by sound reason may go astray, a point that I tried to make clear in my first lecture. In the case of the Manson family, it was not the religious experience per se that led to tragedy but rather the bizarre *interpretation* of the experience that was at fault.

Though I would agree with Malony's statement that religious

experience is influenced by teaching — at least usually — I would deny that there are no native elements. In Mysticism and Philosophy (1960), Stace describes his researches in which he surveyed accounts of mystical experience in all ages and among all faiths, as I have described earlier. His ability to abstract universal characteristics found among mystics with no connection with one another, if it does not prove, suggests a native element to be distinguished from the interpretation of the experience, which is learned.

To support my opinion and since I participated in the experiment, I can testify that the Good Friday subjects were not given mystical categories until several days following the experiment. Furthermore, none of them had yet had the course on mysticism, nor did they know much about it. Yet in the free description of their experiences, spoken into a tape recorder after the service, all of Stace's categories appeared, according to the ratings of independent judges, among one or another of nine out of ten of the subjects who were given the drug and in one of the control subjects to a minor degree. Since psychedelic chemicals elicit only those reactions already resident in the organism, the experiment suggests strong evidence for the existence of a native religious impulse that may be influenced by teaching but is independent of it. It is this impulse that explains also the amazement that overwhelms the subject surprised by a mystical encounter. There is an element of this in conversion experiences, though these latter are much more likely to be triggered by evangelism and teaching.

The needs fulfilled through religious experience may in part be similar to those postulated by the conventional psychological theoretician, in particular the need to find meaning in life. With respect to mysticism, however, the need follows from its native character. It is because the impulse is there that its expression is so captivating. It is not what Maslow (1962) would call a "deficiency" or D-need, but rather a "being" or B-need. The latter are little connected with the D-needs associated with survival, as hunger, thirst, nurturance, etc., but rather are those needs which give life its color, liveliness, and transcendence. The need to experience and produce beauty, to dance, and to play all derive from these obscure native urges to express oneself, which bring delight. More fundamental but akin to this is the immediate experience of ultimate reality, the unity of all things, "the dark silence in which all lovers lose themselves," or simply, God. It is the latter that make up what James calls the "fountainhead" of all religions.

Malony is on sounder ground when he taxes me with omitting to postulate a system of ethics by which to judge behavior. I suppose that implicitly I assumed a system of Christian ethics, though naturally each religion, in interpreting mystical and ecstatic experience in its own way, will bring to bear its own system. Pious Hindus and Buddhists, for example, reverence all life and refuse to take it, while a Christian is unlikely to reflect on where his porterhouse steak comes from or refrain from killing the insect that is biting his nose. But whatever the ethical system, it will bring into play those rational faculties I indicated were so important to be integrated with the nonrational.

I am not so sure what he means when he suggests that I believe in coercion with respect to conversion, for I cannot imagine anything but a superficial change occurring through coercion, as when the Emperor Constantine forced his army to be baptized and converted to Christianity. To require conversion in return for a status privilege, such as membership in a church, invites fakery.

But when Malony explains his concept of coercion as "planning for and controlling a situation" I demur – and this, only mildly – over the term "controlling." I think we have too much of the commodity of ecclesiastical control already, whether in the realm of Christian education or institutional discipline. I know that we need at least some of the latter in any viable institution, but I feel considerably more cheerful over the idea of "planning for" religious experience. Church members should be taught about it, instructed in the lives of worthy exemplars, and given support when the experience comes. But such experience should always be respected in its uniqueness, remembering that it was Jesus who reminded his followers that "the wind bloweth where it listeth and thou hearest the sound thereof, but canst not tell whence it cometh nor whither it goeth; so is everyone that is born of the spirit" (John 3:8). The climate of every creative event must be free. Should this generalization not apply to the most creative event possible in the life of every individual – the encounter with the Holy?

Finally, he asks whether drug methods in acts of worship are viable. Tippett registers an even stronger objection, which I will deal with later. Obviously there would be something wrong with my brains were I not aware of popular attitudes toward drugs – or at least anything *labeled* a drug, for wine has been used immemorially in religious sacraments, even though sometimes in excess in early celebrations of the Lord's Supper and in modern times when there have been cases of alcoholics started on a bout of drunkenness through ingestion of sacramental wine. Such use of a drug is hardly ever criticized, while the hue and cry after the psychedelics, whether used religiously or not, is such that even religious bodies are able to use them only surreptitiously without fear of harrassment and arrest. Even the Indians' traditional use of peyote has been proscribed until very recently.

But as in all events which people recognize as religious, there will be defiance despite legal interdiction (see Clark, 1969). As the Indians have abundantly demonstrated in their use of peyote, properly monitored psychedelic worship services may be not only dignified, but completely safe and an aid both to the spiritual lives and social effectiveness of those who participate. Doubtless the underground religious use of psychedelic drugs by whites will yield experience and guidelines that eventually should emerge as stimuli to the churches.

It is impossible to say just how much influence the drugs have already had on the religious thinking and the lives of the youth, but it is clear that it is very great. This is not to say that the use of the psychedelic drugs is always the best road to the religious life, although there are many, such as Baba Ram Dass, formerly a Harvard professor and now an Indian ascetic, who would have discovered the religious path in no other way. For the churches to neglect this religion of youth without studying it and trying to understand it is folly. From a position of ignorance, they will neither correct its excesses nor come to terms with its more valuable aspects.

REJOINDER TO DAANE

Possibly my differences with Dr. Daane are the most fundamental of all. I have disclaimed the role of Christian apologist not because I am not a Christian but because I do not feel that this is the field of my competency.

Daane complains that I do not present Christianity as unique and distinct from other faiths. It is true that I do not deal with this issue, for I did not see it as important to my task. I agree with Stace and James in seeing the mystical potential of human beings as the *psychological* source of all religions. I do not think that God would single out Christians as the special beneficiaries of psychological capacities denied to members of other faiths. All races and religious groups have the same religious potentialities expressed through their mystical and ecstatic potentialities, the nonrational sources of these powers. But it does not follow that all faiths interpret these or express them alike. Just as each individual is unique in his own way, so is each religious faith and tradition unique.

For me it is the Christian tradition and Jesus Christ to which I give my loyalty and assent, even though that loyalty might not agree at every specific point with certain creeds. And even though history shows me that Christiandom has a far from perfect record, this does not alter my faith that a truer following of Christ is the best hope our world has of saving itself. But certainly this does not blind me to the fact that there are many professing non-Christian men who are more deeply religious than I am, even by the standards of Christ himself.

Though I do not despise the intellectual expression of faith in Jesus Christ, I hold it is much more important to *experience* Him in the depths of our being. I think that Jesus made essentially this same point for me when he singled out a member of the most despised religious group known to his community as an example of what he meant by the term "neighbor" in his parable of the Good Samaritan (Luke 10:25-37).

Furthermore I do not understand Daane when he complains that I do not describe Christian methods of studying the psychology of religion. Even though the phenomenology of this psychology may be unique, as I hold it to be, and therefore may require special methods adapted to the subject matter, this does not depart from rubrics guiding any science. We do not have Christian methods of studying biology or physics. Black is black and two times three equals six no matter what one's faith commitment may be. It is only the *use* to which the findings of psychological science, or any other science, may be put that can be distinguished as Christian. Albert Schweitzer did not take a special course in Christian medicine to prepare for his notable missionary career, though without his Christian motivation it never would have come about.

And even though mysticism is indeed a human potentiality not needing Christ, as both Stace and Otto clearly demonstrate, it does not follow that Christianity or any other faith, for that matter, can develop its full richness without mysticism. This latter conclusion follows most thoroughly and essentially from my often-stated position that *all* faiths are rooted in mysticism. Without it, they become desiccated and feeble, victims of self-indulgent inertia or creatures of power-hungry politicians. I am not denying that mysticism may also lead to fanaticism or the demonic. Here is where it is so important that the nonrational be balanced by rational elements, of which I have spoken.

Christian theology and a Christian system of ethics are examples of two means of supplying these rational elements. They are also means of directing the energies generated by ecstatic experience toward sound thinking and good works. It is true that mystics may make the mistake of quietism, as is evident from some Eastern faiths and communities as well as occasionally in the West also. But such ecstatics as St. Francis, Meister Eckhart, St. Teresa of Avila, St. Catherine of Genoa, George Fox, and John Woolman or even Gautama or Socrates, were not merely shrinking and self-indulgent seekers after an inner bliss but among the most vigorous and influential leaders and doers of good works in history. In their works, the Christians in the list took their cues from Paul of Tarsus, but particularly from Jesus himself.

If what Daane means by my "preaching" is the statement of my belief in such principles as those about which I have been speaking, then I am a preacher. But I do not see these principles as a "theology" but merely the results of my observations as a psychologist. For example, I see the mystical consciousness as psychologically prior to and deeper than the acts and beliefs of any faith, Christianity included. These are the results of my observations and study of the psychology of religion. In this field I have not been uninfluenced by intuitions and "hunches" but no more so than any other psychologist, and certainly not as much as was the case with my distinguished predecessor, William James, who has influenced my thinking so much.

Since I have learned never to rely solely on those reputed to be authorities, I have tried to put these intuitions to the test whenever I could, always preferring my own observations and experiments whenever that was possible. I have then subjected these data to a systematic review resulting not in any final view of truth but tentative conclusions to be subjected to further study. This seems to me to be psychology, not theology, though I must thank Daane for the implied compliment in proposing me for inclusion in such august company as the theologians.

REJOINDER TO TIPPETT

I find myself in closest agreement with the comments of Tippett, perhaps because he spelled out his points of agreement with me, and so I feel myself better able to enter into dialogue with him in order to answer some of his criticisms. Then, he and I agree on the need for more emphasis on the mystical elements in religion, which I hold so important.

The first considerable difference lies in his intuitive suspicion of the value and appropriateness of drugs as an agent of religious experience. I have no difficulty in empathizing with this feeling, for it was my own before I had learned very much about the psychedelics through firsthand observation and experiment. Even now, I feel that a good deal of caution should be exercised as well as a proper respect for the task in hand. I do not deny that the psychedelics may be abused or used for escape, or that there are not certain dangers involved with their use. All that I can say is that from my own study and follow-up, when the drugs are used religiously, abuse is minimal and the rewards are often very great.

As already indicated, I was myself present in a supervisory capacity at the Good Friday experiment. I can testify that few services I have attended have been more reverent or impressive. Typical among the volunteers was one of the most conservative and deeply religious students at Andover Newton Theological School, with whom I afterward discussed the event. He had attended out of curiosity, but the religious intent of the experimenters so impressed him that he volunteered and counted himself richly rewarded in having the good fortune to draw one of the psychedelic capsules.

Also, I have mentioned participating in an Indian peyote ceremony. It was the most impressive religious ceremony I have ever attended, thanks to my ingestion of the sacrament. Despite its syncretic nature, the ceremony was clearly Christian oriented. I felt a solidarity with my Indian brothers and sisters remarkable in its depth. Doubtless there were differing intellectual interpretations of the various aspects of the ceremony among the 5 whites and 15 Indians present, though I did not sense that they were any greater than with most of the many more conventional Christian services that, according to my custom, I regularly attend. I do not present these instances as the proof of anything but simply as a piece of personal testimony to the effect that for me, at least, neither of these two services seemed either unnatural or overcontrolled.

I am not troubled over the fact that there is no scriptural authority for the use of the psychedelics, though the English scholar John Allegro and others have suggested that psychedelic herbs may have had a place in biblical ecstatic experiences and worship. I see the drugs simply as tools comparable to the loudspeaker often used in Christian worship, similarly lacking in biblical sanction. To me the problem is how the tools are used. If, as seems to be the case with peyote cults, drugs are used to help worshippers face their problems, love one another, and live more effective lives, then their use is justified. If, as is the case frequently with the Jivaro Indians in Ecuador, the use of the psychedelic ayahuasca is enlisted to harm enemies or to assist in head- hunting, one could see this as a demonic use of the drug. As in the case of other uses of powerful drugs, the religious use of the psychedelics must be studied with an open but critical mind. Tippett's statement that there is no scriptural authority for the use of any drug is not quite accurate, for there is. The drug I am referring to, of course, is alcohol, product of fermentation present in wine.

Dr. Tippett has inquired about the criteria I used in my survey of LSD-type drug users justifying my statements that 76 per cent experienced "the Holy" and 78 per cent, "psychological rebirth." These were gathered from the replies on a questionnaire from subjects who had such drugs. On 30 or more categories supplied on the questionnaires, the subjects were asked to compare their drug experiences with their normal or everyday experiences and then rate them from 0 to 5, with 0 representing "no different from normal" to 5 representing "beyond anything experienced or imagined." The percentages I reported gave ratings of 1 or better, with nearly two thirds of the sample further indicating that their experiences were intense and nearly one third reporting them "beyond anything experienced or imagined" in their previous ordinary lives. In such subjective reports, there is no way of comparing one with another any more than there is of knowing to what degree those who say they have had an experience of God are speaking of the same thing.

What we can be sure of is that many are speaking of a very intense experience that went far beyond anything known to them in their normal states of consciousness, and that religious language frequently comes closest to enabling them to report what has happened to them. A convinced atheist does not readily acknowledge that he has "met God," and yet I have known this to happen several times to atheists among my circle of acquaintances who have used the psychedelics. In every case, this was followed by a heightening and an integration of purpose in living and concern for others.

As a researcher, I can do no other than to approach as closely as I can to those who use the drugs religiously to observe, to empathize, to participate when my conscience will allow me to, and to come to what appear to me to be responsible conclusions.

I think we underestimate the influence of the psychedelic drugs in our religion and our culture. Because their use is underground and out of sight, we tend to identify their use with the most irresponsible and disreputable elements of the youth culture. We have made them illegal and then tried to justify that illegality by a wild exaggeration of their dangers and a refusal to acknowledge their uses. Since the youth who use them see through these untruths, this widens the communication gap and closes minds of the other side to truths spoken now by youth and now by age.

I do not think that the road to transcendence through drugs is the best source of the religious consciousness. Even when they are used responsibly, I seem to notice that their best exponents use them sparingly and tend to replace them by other methods of stirring the mystical consciousness over the years. But I do think that there are many Americans who either will be introduced to mysticism by this method or not at all. My conviction is that it is far better for them to start off this way than not at all, and I believe that it is essential that the churches mend the poverty of their spiritual foundations by some means or manner. I hope I am wrong when I fear that they may lack the courage to face the ordeal of an honest facing of the facts about these drugs and a thorough testing of both their values and their dangers. It is here that there is great need of that balance between the nonrational and rational elements in religion, of which I have spoken.

Particularly in Tippett's discussion of conversion and his recognition of the need for the good missionary to recognize the positive values of those he wishes to convert, I perceive him to be a Christian of broad human sympathy and understanding. At the very least, if we are going to appreciate and guide the youth of our counterculture, this requires that we get close to them so that we may understand their undoubted positive virtues. We want to use these virtues at the same time so that we may help the young people to avoid their many mistakes. In their concern for the spiritual life, they may lie ready to supply to the churches and the religious resources of our culture those elements of which we stand in greatest need. We cannot close our eyes to the fact that so many of them testify to the psychedelics being agents of great religious significance in our time.

But I must turn to another of Tippett's criticisms which I must acknowledge as cogent: in his complaint that I have largely neglected the social element in religious experience, he is on sound ground. I have more or less deliberately focussed on the psychology of the individual, in part because I have not had time to take up eveything but, more importantly, by way of under-lining my conviction that religion starts with the religious experience of the *individual.*

It is true that religious experience is always to some degree influenced by the individual's social *milieu.* But the upwelling of that experience, particularly among our greatest prophets, or in us ourselves in our most intense encounters with the Holy, has so often occurred when the individual in some sense is alone — Socrates before Potidea, Moses in the wilderness or on the slopes of Sinai, Francis or Loyola in their hours of sickness, George Fox wandering in the woods clothed in his suit of leather, or Jesus in his moments of withdrawl from the crowds. All of these suggest a source of power buried deeply within the self. We must begin at the beginning of things, and it is my conviction, in company with James, quoted above, that it is with the individual that religion begins.

With respect to what the place of theology and belief might be in the religious scheme of things, my disposition is to give them a lower position than does Tippett. In other words I would hold that an *experience* of Christ is much more important than simple a *belief* in Him, insofar as the latter is a mere intellectual assent. The deeper the perceptive roots of the experience, the greater its durability will be. However, I acknowledge that a religion made up wholly of roots would be no more impressive than a tree in the same condition. Religion is no sooner experienced than it must be interpreted intellectually, cither to oneself or to others. Further-more, it begins to take on implications for living. Here is where theology, ethics, and church structure begin to take form, and the differentiation between faiths begins to evolve.

Even though I prefer Christianity and see Christ as the source of my own particular loyalty, direction, and inspiration, I would be blind not to acknowledge that "correct" theology and thinking about Christ will not save me or others from demonic distortion of the teachings of the gentle Nazarene. For what else than demonic were the excesses of the Inquisition, certain aspects of the

Crusades, and the European wars for political supremacy in the names of various forms of the Christian faith in Europe following the Reformation. One does not have to depart from scenes of our own day, as in Northern Ireland and elsewhere, to sense a departure from the teachings of Christ that are demonic in the sense of justifying extremes of violence and cruelty in the name of Christ. While such aberrations may be in part correctible through reason, I suspect that a sense of their sinfulness ultimately will be traced back to obscure internal processes in which a mystical encounter with the divine ground of all Being will have an essential place.

It is in this sense that I ventured to express my convictions about the brotherhood of all men. There *are* ways, and these are very profound and basic, in which all men are brothers. In our competitive generation, obsessed with security and the consequent national craving for power and other material values, we have lost awareness of that brotherhood except for a very narrow circle of family and close friends. Mankind has been transformed into potential competitors or enemies. In a technological world with its fast-developing means of mass slaughter, to hide from ourselves the essential oneness of man is a delusion we cannot maintain and still survive. Only some means of enabling us to experience ourselves and one another at that depth of selfhood where we are one will save mankind from itself.

My statement that it is only through the mystical consciousness that brotherhood may be universally realized was made against the background of such considerations. It is a statement of possibility and hope, not proof. It is an intuition but also a deep faith which has achieved persuasiveness subjectively as the conviction has grown within me over the years. It is a kind of a pointing of the way which leaves many details to be added and many gaps to be filled in, and therefore I must state it as a kind of preaching or exhortation, as Daane has reminded me. It is a venture of faith at the same time it is a counsel of desperation in a time of danger where intelligence, world organization, good intentions, churchly religion, and moral exhortation are not enough.

At the same time that this conviction is an unproved intuition, it is not completely without its plausibility and supporting evidence. Most persuasively there is the immediate perception reported by practically all mystics that the universe is one. It follows that all mankind is one, and the compassion and sense of kinship with others developed by the mystics supports and confirms this perception. I have found evidences of such development in my researches into the characteristics and dynamics of mystical experience released by the psychedelics. In two cases this empathy included even noxious insects, which the subjects found themselves unable to kill for several months following their experiences. We know that the sympathies of St. Francis began with people, extended to the birds of the air and even to "Brother Wolf."

The firmest bases in motivation for the observation of any system of ethics, personal or international, is not simply that of the Golden Rule. We may try to do unto others what we would like them to do unto us partly as a means of self protection, a motive that is bound to break down amid the complexity of modern living. The immediate realization that the welfare of others is our own welfare lays a far more durable base for social living and is probably the *only* viable motive for ethics.

I do not know that, in fact, enough men will see this truth and act on it. But I do feel strongly that it is not just the religious elite who have the capacity for mystical ecstasy. Mysticism is only out of fashion, just as art and music and poetry tend to be among ordinary folk. It is the need for the artist, whether secular or religious, that can bring out his expression in any one of us. There are few of us who have not been poets, at least to some degree, when we were in love. In the same way we fall in love with God through mystical ecstasy when the need of Him is great enough, for the opportunity is always there.

There are many ways in which the psychologist of religion may liken the religious life to the secular life about him and study it accordingly. But it is the transcendental mystical dimension of religion that is unique and distinguishes religion from all other human activity. And it is only an activity with the force and the depth of the mystical consciousness that can hope to transform our sick society.

There remains only one more of Tippett's points that I would like to reply to. In alluding to the common element in all religions, he speaks of a "lowest common denominator." I would not necessarily see a common element in *all* so-called religions, high and low, for I do acknowledge the existence of what would seem to be either "demonic" religions or religions in which the chief element is demonic. I would not see these as pointing toward the brotherhood of man. But I do think that the roots of all of the *great* faiths are mystical. The common denominator in these faiths I would see not so much as a lowest one but a denominator that is highest.

For it would be this highest element, deriving its sense of brotherhood from a sense of unity possible because of the common origin of all men in what *we Christians* call God. The Interpreter on whom we rely as One closest to God is Christ, and through the Holy Spirit each of us is enabled directly to experience both Christ and God. Thus each of us partakes in some way of both Christ and God, even though, paradoxically, we may at the same time dwell at an infinite distance from each.

It was Meister Eckhart, the great Christian mystic, who experienced this oneness. Yet posthumously he was declared a heretic by the Roman Catholic Church, at that time overpunctilious in its concern for logical categories and perhaps also too amenable to the influence of divisive political factions within its walls. But it was his sense of the Ground of our common source and his direct experience of Christ that led Eckhart to regard all men as his brothers and to recognize the priority of the need of his brother even over his participation in the mystical ecstasy that so moved him.

In connection with a discussion of the meaning of his concept of the "new man in Christ," I once asked Paul Tillich who would be the better Christian — one who accepted every jot and tittle of the strait and narrow line of complete Christian orthodoxy but who was mean and self-centered in his dealings with others, or a pagan whose grace and loving spontaneous generosity accepted the claims of his neighbor as co-equal with his own. His reply was that the pagan would be a "new man in Christ," or one whose personality was fashioned by the standards of Christ. To me this was what Jesus was saying when he told the parable of the Good

Samaritan. It was attitude and deeds, not orthodoxy, that was crucial. As a goal for all religions, this is not a "least common denominator," but a denominator without which neither domestic nor international peace is possible.

I do not maintain that such a result is invariably the product of mystical experience, for the living of a full religious life requires much more than simply the mystical consciousness. Neither do I hold that a large minded and generous attitude is only to be found among mystics. What I am saying is that, generally speaking, there is no transforming and creative source of compassion and concern for one's neighbor equal to mysticism. Furthermore, it is the only source that is deeply and characteristically religious. I do not believe that life on our planet will long be viable without a quickening of this ecstatic and transforming source of good will and love.

REFERENCES

Allen, G. W.: William James: A biography. New York, Viking Press, 1967.

Allport, G.: Use of personal documents in psychological science, 1942.

Clark, W. H.: Chemical ecstasy. New York, Sheed & Ward, 1969, pp. 135-153.

Clark, W. H.: The Oxford Group: Its history and significance. New York, Bookman Associates, 1951.

James, W.: The varieties of religious experience. New York, New American Library, 1961.

Maslow, A. H.: Toward a psychology of being. Princeton, N. J., Van Nostrand, 1962.

Pahnke, W. N.: Drugs and mysticism: An analysis of the relationship between mystical consciousness and psychedelic drugs. Harvard University Ph.D. dissertation, 1964.

Perry, R. B.: The thought and character of William James. New York, Braziller, 1954.

Stace, W. J.: Mysticism and philosophy. Philadelphia, Lippincott, 1960.

QUESTIONS AND ANSWERS TO
LECTURES BY
WALTER HOUSTON CLARK

Discussion # 1
February 1, 1971

Q: Paul Tillich has said that in Christian education we teach our children the answers long before they know how to ask the questions. This seems to imply that there is somewhat of a rational basis to all religious experience and more explicitly implying that when a person has a religious experience it actually is an answer to a legitimate perhaps even rational question. How does this relate to your seeming implication that the nonrational precedes or goes before the rational?

A: I would say that there always is a certain amount of dialogue that is occurring. Nevertheless, a child comes into the world as a nonrational creature with no language. And of course it is very well known that religion starts with birth and that some of the most important moments of the child are those hours right after he comes into the world. Therefore I would say that the earlier the child gets his instruction, whether rational or nonrational, the more effective it is. And I think that just because the nonrational is more primitive, it must come first.

Q: Dr. Clark has said that the LSD type of drug produces religious experiences, meaning I guess that we knew about religious experiences before the drug. In other words, we must have known there were some things called religious experiences and now when the drug affects somebody, the effect is similar to what we had been calling, or what we knew as religious experience. Does the drug produce the experience or does it elicit it?

129

A: You are getting me ahead of myself, Lee, because I'm going to deal with this problem in the next lecture, but let me answer that briefly right now. I look on the drugs as I look on the developer of photographic film. All the developer does is to bring out a picture that is already there that you can't see. And therefore I am always very careful when I talk about these drugs to refer to them as triggers, developers, or releasers of religious experience. And of course they're not the only triggers, because there are many others, as I will try to describe tomorrow.

Q: Comment about the harmfulness of these drugs.

A: Well I don't think there is any need for me to talk about the harmfulness of these drugs because you can read that in any paper. But I might say that in my opinion, the harmfulness of the drugs has been greatly exaggerated. In my own experience with them, and I suppose I have guided 150 trips on the drugs in connection with scientific studies, I am amazed that such powerful drugs can be so comparatively safe. Now that doesn't mean that I don't think that they are dangerous, because even if one per cent of what we're told about their dangers were true, they would still remain dangerous. Of their dangers first I might point out that if an improper person takes the drugs — let's say a borderline psychotic — he may be pushed over the edge. Especially if he takes them supervised by a person who isn't very well experienced with the drugs, he is much more likely to get in trouble than he is if somebody gives him the drugs who is well acquainted with them. For example, I know of a hospital in Canada where they administered these drugs twelve hundred times, and they've never come across any problems that they couldn't readily handle. Here I should say that they are careful to screen people that take drugs. Second, there is the danger that an occasional subject will try to jump from a great height or pass through a speeding car. And so my own feeling is that, only if these drugs are administered by people who know their business, are they safe. Here I would not include just any doctor or any psychiatrist that wanted to administer them. The guide requires special training and experience. But I'm amazed in my researches, in the one hundred people that I surveyed carefully, so far as I could tell from their subjective responses, there was only one that seemed to have come to any long-lasting, harm, and I'm not sure that even that was *very* long lasting, and it came from indiscriminate use of not just the psychedelics. So in summary, let me say that I think the dangers of the drugs have been over emphasized, their possible usefulness has been under emphasized, and I hope that as time goes on, we will be much freer to have competent people who know their business experimenting with the drugs. In this way we will know more precisely in what respect the drugs are harmful and in what other respects they have possible uses — perhaps revolutionary uses, in the field of mental health and also in religion. In the latter, the Indians already seem to have shown us the way.

Q: Comment on the parallels between a drug-induced mystical experience and the experience of speaking in tongues.

A: I think there are a great many parallels. I would say that the drugs are one trigger for the release of mystical experience. I think that speaking in tongues is another trigger, or perhaps the trigger is something else, but the speaking in tongues is part of the phenomena associated often times with mystical experience. However, I must admit that I know less about speaking in tongues than I do about the drugs where I have personally done investigations and observed what happens and then systematically tried put together the data that I have discovered. But both tend to mark ecstatic experiences and that's what I'm talking about in these lectures. I'll have a little more to say about speaking in tongues in a subsequent lecture.

Q: Would you compare a psychedelic trip and drunkenness?

A: I would compare them only in the sense that they are both drug induced. I'm sorry to say that I'm not an expert in drunkenness, never having been drunk. I have had a little experience with LSD. That's maybe one of the reasons why I can always get off the hook at a cocktail party. When I'm offered a drink, I can always say that I never take anything stronger than

LSD. I always get a laugh, and the funny thing about it is that I believe it. I don't think that we are in nearly as much danger with our use of LSD-type drugs as we are with alcohol. But neverthe-.less, I've had to rely on what other people tell me about drunkenness, and those that are experts in both fields say that one is not at all like the other. When you take alcohol, your sensitivities are benumbed and your alertness is reduced whereas in taking LSD, your perceptions are increased. You're made more alert, more sensitive: more sensitive to music, more sensitive to beauty of other kinds, more sensitive to that religious capacity which is sleeping within all of us. I would say that the effect of the two is contradictory. And of course this is one of the problems, I think, in the public's misunderstanding of the psychedelics. They assume that they are like alcohol. And we have so many experts in the effects of alcohol in our society who come to the erroneous conclusion that taking the psychedelic drugs must be the same thing. But one of our problems here is the lack of discrimination, the lack of clear understanding of what these drugs do.

Q: I've often wondered if the experiences now in your current research being described as religious experiences might be a way of understanding the New Testament, and perhaps the experience of the Revelation in the New Testament might also be revelations possible within human experience today. Do you see the uniqueness of the New Testament to be so that it is impossible to make a parallel, or do you see a bridge here?

A: Your question, as I understand it, is do these researches with the drugs help us to understand better the psychology of the New Testament, the Bible? I would say definitely yes. I have had many biblical passages clarified for me by my own experience. I have a very good friend who participated with me in one of my experiments who is a very noted biblical scholar. After his experience he wanted to study the protocols of people that had taken the drugs for the light that they would throw on the psychology of the prophets. His application for a grant to do this very promising study, unfortunately, was turned down.

Discussion # 2
February 2, 1971

Q: Can the mystical experience occur without moral counterparts or are the two connected in any way?

A: Stace, in the last chapter in his book, entertains the theory that the mystical experience is the basis for a truly moral life. If one has an experience of unity, where one finds his identity with all living things, then he gets to the place where he can love his enemy, when he doesn't need to inquire for whom the bell tolls because he knows that it tolls for him and for every man. This is the very basis of morality, and I think that you find, certainly in the Christian mystical tradition and other traditions as well, that there is a high relationship between moral behavior and mystical experience. Meister Eckhart, for example, when somebody asked him in effect this same question — what would happen if somebody in need came to him during a vision, a mystical visition? — replied that it would be far better for the mystic to leave his vision and to satisfy his neighbor's need and then return to his vision.

Of course there is always the problem that mystics get sidetracked, get fascinated with their visions and begin to enjoy them for their own sake. Thus, in the Middle Ages there grew up what was labeled a heresy, the heresy of "quietism," where people who made too much of mysticism could do nothing else and couldn't show the fruits that Jesus said would distinguish wholesome from unwholesome religion. The great mystics have always tied mysticism to some kind of moral purpose. Also, we find that the great mystics are capable of very clear thinking, Mathematicians are particulary susceptible to mystical experience, yet you might think that these would be the last people who would be. But Einstein was mystic; Pascal, one of the keenest French thinkers of all times, was also a mystic; there was Kepler, the astronomer, Sir Isaac Newton, and even Bertrand Russell. The latter said there were two things important in the world. One was science and the other was mysticism. And, of course, Bertrand

Russell, whether you agree with him or not, had a very keen sense of social responsibility and ethics. So my answer very clearly is that wholesome mysticism is a responsible mysticism, is a responsible thing socially. It is allied both with clear thinking and social responsibility.

Q: What are the correct criteria for the correct interpretation of the mystical experience?

A: Personally I prefer the criteria developed by W.T. Stace, though James, Underhill, and Otto will all help us. The central feature of mysticism is the experience of unity, around which other characteristics may be seen to cluster. Though it is very desirable to have accounts from practical mystics, like Underhill and Otto, nevertheless there is always the danger that these will tend to overgeneralize subjective aspects of their own experiences.

Q: Did Paul unnecessarily restrict himself when he said, I preach Christ crucified, or could he have made it a broader approach to the problems of humanity?

A: Paul, like any other mystic, had to have an interpretation of his experience, and this is his interpretation, the way he preferred to describe the experience. I speak to you as a prejudiced person, a person prejudiced in favor of the Christian interpretation of mysticism, and I can imagine no broader application than the application that my understanding of Christ suggests. But nonetheless, were Paul brought up in a completely different tradition, a Hindu or Buddhist tradition, then I expect that probably he would have used a Hindu or Buddhist interpretation. Although I prefer Christian interpretations because of my Christian provincialism, if you want to call it that, nevertheless I could respect others. I believe Christians will profit from a study of them. And I don't think that we can help respecting people like Socrates, Gantama, and other mystics – spiritual giants in other traditions.

Q: Dr. Clark, a sociologist, Morton, has combined work with a psychologist, King, at Southern Methodist University in factor analyzing religiosity as such, and I'm puzzled as to why no one of the factors seems to refer to mysticism as such.

A: Frankly, you find some psychologists of religion that have very little use for mysticism. Some of these people are good friends of mine, but I think that they just haven't penetrated deeply enough into the nature of religion. In their disagreement, they would feel that maybe I was involving myself in ideas that are too esoteric.

But I cannot comment on the study you mention, since I am not familiar with it. Factor analyses derive from a study only what is put into them. Perhaps mystical elements were not included in the original data under study.

Q: How old do you have to be to have a mystical experience, and what evidence is there for mystical experiences in childhood?

A: I think that the foundations of mystical experiences frequently are in childhood, and maybe this is what Jesus was trying to tell us when he said that we had to be like little children if we wanted to enter the kingdom of Heaven. There is a kind of a surrender on the part of the child, a feeling for mystery, and a giving up of themselves to things that are bigger than themselves. I'm sure that the roots of mystical experience are to be found in childhood. In the time of William Wordsworth, they used to feel that the most wholesome form of personality was that found in a little child.

On the other hand, there are certain complexities of growth and certain ripenings that come, so that as the child gets older, his capacity for a richer mystical experience grows. Or it may be that in a sense a mystical experience in older people is a kind of regression. Fingarette speaks of "regression in the service of the ego." In other words, the adult, in a sense, goes back to the birth experience and has a second chance. He grows up again with the benefit of all the accretions that have entered his personality; so that while I would hesitate to say that the child can have a fully developed mystical experience, nevertheless I'm quite certain that the roots of mystical experience are very importantly to be found in the children and in how the children are treated. But mysticism can came at any age — the richer the personality the more productive the mysticism.

Q: Have the empirical results of your research added to or supported Stace's criteria?

A: Well, I have not found any data which has been entirely fresh, new, and original. But I think that one can easily modify Stace's characteristics by certain suggestions of other students of mysticism, particularly Rudolf Otto. In Stace, we find very little said about the *mysterium tremendum,* about awe. And in mystical experience, very often, and ecstasy of many kinds, we have an experience of fear, an experience perhaps of reverence associated with fear, that we call awe. This is one of the weaknesses of Stace. In my researches, when I have asked about experiences of fear of one kind or another, I find that people who use the psychedelic drugs often mention these. When we look at great religious personalities such as Moses, we find fear, as when Moses stood before the burning bush, or Abram when he experienced "an horror of great darkness." So here is where I would tend to modify Stace, not from anything original, but from ideas that come from Rudolf Otto. I'm sure that one can find still other criteria that can modify Stace's, but I think that for a clear-cut definition and description of mysticism, it's pretty hard to find anything better than Stace. He is so incisive in his description. He's not easy reading, but he is very clear and very perceptive. My researchers give considerable support to his criteria.

Q: What is the relationship between abnormal and normal mysticism; and how might mysticism relate to abnormal psychology, and more specifically schizophrenia and its treatment and diagnosis?

A: The relationship between abnormal and normal mysticism is partly a matter of definition. Some psychiatrists would see all mysticism as abnormal. If you have read much in Thomas Szaz or R. D. Laing, you have been introduced to the problem of how dubious many of our concepts of the abnormal are. Doubtless many mystics have been transformed into patients by well-meaning psychiatrists who have no idea what a mystical experience is. I am sure that St. Anthony or George Fox, were they alive today and unfortunate enough to be committed to the typical mental hospital, would be relegated to the back wards and the world would be deprived of two creative religious leaders.

In his excellent modern text on personality, *THE PERSONAL WORLD,* Harold G. McCurdy shows himself to be aware of the problem to which I have alluded. In his discussion of mysticism, he gives the account of the distinguished psychiatrist, Pierre Janet, and ecstatic patient, Madeleine, given to trances and uttering of prophecies, at the Salpetriere Hospital in Paris (McCurdy, 1961, pp. 496-502). In her mystical ecstasies, Madeleine experienced the love of God, which so possessed her that it overflowed into love for other patients and supported her resolution to pattern her life after Francis of Assisi. To the great Janet, she was hardly more than another case, though a very interesting one. The results of her ecstatic states — "hallucinations" to Janet — were that she lived a life of poverty, austerity, and good works, both in the hospital and after she got out. McCurdy presents both the position of the uncomprehending psychiatrist who, from his lofty pinnacle, sees Madeleine's ecstasies simply as the expressions of bodily processes gone wrong; and Madeleine, whose mystical ecstasies and the love engendered by them within her seem the gifts of God. McCurdy poses the question, Who was right, Janet or Madeleine, the psychiatrist or the mystic?

This is not to say that I do not believe there is such a thing as a psychotic state, an extreme denial of life's problems in schizophrenic withdrawal. I might even accept, tentatively, the proposition that some mystics tend to become schizophrenic, since the roots of mystical perceptions and certain personality problems often exist at about the same depth within the psyche. But I do believe that a psychiatrist or psychologist with some understanding of the power and nature of mystical states of consciousness, and the gift of understanding and compassion, may help psychotics to make the most of their psychotic episodes, perhaps as constructively and creatively as Madeleine. This is about as much as I can say this time about this important and complex question.

Discussion # 3
February 3, 1971

Q: Dr. Clark, I wonder if you have seen the recent issue of *Look* magazine which reports on a movement here in southern California, particularly at a church which I am acquainted with in Costa Mesa. There, in contrast to some of the things you have said about the effects of psychedelic drugs, these young people seem to be substituting a religious experience for the drug experience and in fact proclaiming that their new experience of Christ saves them from drugs. I wonder how you would accord that with some of the things you have said.

A: Of course, the drugs have a very bad name, and I think the assumption of the average American is that people need to be saved from these evil instruments. I look on the drugs as tools which, like automobiles, can be abused and when abused can be very dangerous, but they also can be used properly. However, I don't think that it's too important whether these young people were started in their religious experiences through a reaction against the drugs. I don't object to that, providing they substitute for it something equally vigorous which they will find they have to follow up and discipline themselves with. The important thing is the religious experience, how durable and how lasting it is, not how it comes about.

Q: Have you done research with sensitivity groups and the possibility of their being triggers for religious experience?

A: I'm not an expert of sensitivity groups, but I'm pretty sure that they are among the triggers, and very wholesome triggers, when they are used properly. I think that, like anything of this sort, they can be misused. They are a very new and very hopeful means of increasing people's religious awareness as well as just their ordinary personal awareness — awareness of other people and their needs.

Q: Do the psychedelic drugs produce a sustaining religious

experience, or is this an experience severed from normal ongoing experience?

A: It depends on the person and what he does with it. If he has a little background, he realizes that one has to keep these experiences and the idealism that comes from them fresh by some sort of activity. In the case of the convict that I told you about, he got his ongoing activity through the organization that he and some of his friends, who also had had the drug, started within the prison gates. I'm sure that a very powerful source of his remaining away from crime was the pride that he took in this group and the discipline that went along with it. On the other hand, – and I've inquired about this – he says that he can't imagine that this change could have taken place without the drugs.

Then I can think of another person, an athiest, who was a volunteer in a research project of which I was one of the research team. He also had a religious experience, an embarrassment, I suppose. A year or so later, I asked him what he felt the drug experience had done for him. "Well," he said, "I thought when I left the hospital that this would be all. I could look back on it as I look back on my college career and college degree. I could forget everything that I'd learned and go out and do other things that were interesting." "But," he said, "I found out that this was just the beginning, and I have been changing and I have been working on this experience ever since."

You have people like these two on the one hand; then on the other hand, a great many of the kids who take the drugs so casually are wasting the possibility of the drugs. And these people, I'm sure, can perhaps use these same experiences as a means of escape from life. Thus one must be critical and has to discriminate between individuals and how they use the drugs. The good and the bad must be balanced against one another.

Q: In the light of the fact that the drug experience is so socially unacceptable, what do we do to induce the obviously valuable mystical experiences?

A: People are so ignorant about these drugs, their attitudes so

distorted, and our laws about them are so benighted, that it is hard
to see any legal opportunities to do the required experimentation.
On the other hand, sometimes things that are valuable and at one
time in history illegal in one way or another do finally push their
way through and are recognized because people are willing to risk
their reputations for something they believe in very strongly.

Let me give you an illustration of that. In the eighteenth
century, it was illegal to use dissection in the medical schools, but
progressive-minded doctors felt that this was the only way that
they'd learn to operate on people. As a result of this, there grew
up the disreputable trade of grave robbing, which one can't but
feel somewhat ambivalent about. And yet I think that any of us
who have ever been under the surgeon's knife are grateful that
some of the doctors and surgeons of those days took their
reputations in their hands in order to pursue the illegal practice of
dissection. Something in a slightly different category was the
Copernican theory during the time of the Inquisition, when even
to look through Galileo's telescope was one of the riskiest things
that one could do, and no respectable scholar who valued his place
in his profession or his university would be found looking through
this telescope.

We face similar dilemmas today. I see young people carelessly
using drugs. I can see how much waste there is of substances that
might be used properly and very valuably, and here youth are
using them in such a way as to maximize the dangers and minimize
the benefits. I can't approve of this sort of thing. And yet there is
another part of me, which knows people who have used these
drugs illegally and have immensely benefited from them. And this
is what makes me ambivalent. Half of me wants these people to be
successful in forcing the law to recognize that there are responsible
ways of using the drugs. The other half disapproves.

But there is no part of me that does not want to see the
psychedelics used by responsible and well-trained psychologists
and physicians, those who have taken the drugs themselves and
understand both their power and their values. And I would like to
see the drugs used religiously, as in the case of the Peyote Indians.
I really haven't any very clear answer to your question except in
terms of an ideal situation, which is not with us. But nevertheless,

very definitely, I think our seminaries have a responsibility to experiment and to give instruction in this whole field of the techniques of profound religious experience, including the psychedelics, whenever this is possible.

Q: Is controlled use of drugs predictable and beneficial?

A: On the whole, very definitely yes. From my study of these drugs, I've found much more evidence of growth on the part of users than I have of harm. Now that doesn't mean that I think that there's no harm, nor that I think that they shouldn't be used very carefully. But I know that whenever they are given by people who know their business, certainly ninety-nine out of one hundred are very glad that they have taken the drug, even those who take it under situations that aren't very ideal. This is one predictability. Another is that there is little hard evidence of genetic damage when the drugs are pure (see Dishotsky *et al.*, 1971). A third predictability is that there are few problems connected with properly conducted experiments (see Cohen, 1960).

Q: Is there any harm that might result from naturally induced mystical experiences?

A: I think there's always danger in any profound religious experience. Anything that releases forces from the unconscious, as you well know, involves a certain amount of risk. And I think that one has to face that, if one is to protect the people, or better, if they are going to protect themselves. Yet the God-possessed person is not interested in protecting himself — rather only in facing God and doing His will. Even though he knows the risk, he will risk all for God.

Q: Can you, as a psychologist, distinguish between one type of experience that would lead a man into AA, say, and another that leads him to become a member of the Pentecostal Church? Can you distinguish either as a psychologist or as a Christian man?

A: My feeling is that psychologically, these experiences are quite similar. They are two ways to the same thing. I think that one can demonstrate that when this sort of experience involves religion — and of course AA does involve religion — they tend to be equally effective. Any cure for alcoholics that involves religion has a tendency — I wouldn't say in every single case — but it has a tendency to be more effective than methods that don't involve this. Religion, particularly in the light of such experiences as I've been talking about, stirs up certain changes from deep within the unconscious, and these have more power and more vigor; therefore they are apt to last longer. I think this is the very nature of religion, whether Christian religion or other forms of religion. However, to answer your question more directly, I have not had enough experience in the field of alcoholism to predict who would be attracted to AA and who to Pentecostalism.

Q: Were the results of the Good Friday Experiment real mysticism and what do you think of Allegro's, *Mushroom and the Cross,* and the writings of R. D. Laing?

A: Let me start with the last ones first because I can remember them. Yes, I am acquainted with Laing's writing and his *Politics of Experience*, whose last chapter is quite clearly a description of his own psychedelic trip. It doesn't say so in the book, but one can see that, and I happen to know that he uses these drugs in his practice and that he has taken them himself, as any responsible psychiatrist that wanted to use the drugs should do. I think rather highly of Laing's writings, although that doesn't mean that I would agree with all of his ideas. Now with respect to Allegro's book, I've read that too. I'm a little ambivalent about the book. I think that what he has suggested is at least a creative speculation relative to many of the things in the Bible. However, the book is mostly linguistic in its approach, and I'm not enough of a linguist to be able to pass on that. I've asked some of my friends who know more about it than I do, and they don't seem to have the highest respect for Allegro. Then another thing that I noticed in the book is that he doesn't seem to know as much about the effects of the drugs, which I should think might be the strongest argument towards establishing its plausibility. Therefore, my attitude toward the book is somewhat on the critical side. Maybe somebody will take his very imaginative ideas and put them on a more solid basis.

Now, for the other part of your question. In Pahnke's Good Friday experiment, there seemed to be no way you could distinguish between the kind of mystical experience that Pahnke's subjects reported and the experience that might have come through more natural methods. Again, what do we mean by a "natural" way of having a mystical experience? If one sets out deliberately to seek such an experience, that in itself is somewhat artificial — including the use of incense; the use of fasting, which is another way to change the biochemical content of the body; the Gregorian chant, and so on and so on. All of these are artificial ways of establishing or at least triggering the mystical experience, which most people accept because they're used to them and they seem "natural" to them. But presumably the first time they were used, they were criticized by some people who said, "You just have to wait on God!" But there's no doubt whatsoever that there are certain things that one can do to prepare for these experiences that make them more likely. So my answer is that I can't tell the differences between these drug-induced mystical experiences and the non-drug-induced. Drugs are just another trigger. W. T. Stace, when he was asked this same question — Is the drug induced experience like mysticism? — replied, "It is not *like* mysticism, it *is* mysticism!" Until contrary evidence has been brought to me, I would agree with this position.

Q: You talk about the importance of structure and dynamics, but you don't tie them together very often. Why does it seem to me that you talk a lot about mysticism and mystical experience, but you don't tie it in very closely with revelation, with the kind of experience which is profitable and leads to wholeness?

A: Well, of course I think it seems that way because I have been emphasizing the ecstatic and the experiencial nature of religion. However, certainly one of the things that one must do in the first place is to open one's eyes to whatever risks of experience there are so that if one takes a risk, it is a calculated one. It is structure that supplies the values and standards for the calculation. Now the Church is one source of structure; here is one place where structure may come into play. And then, of course, along with Church structure, a person engages in activities as a Christian, such as the Christian disciplines of studying the Bible, of reading the Gospels, and absorbing as much as possible a feeling for the personality of Christ. These can be used as guidelines in evaluating the mystical experience. These are some of the elements of structure I would emphasize.

Q: My first question has to do with your own pilgrimage in relating psychology and religion, and the second has to do with tying in some of the methodology concerns of psychology such as behaviorism and functionalism with an understanding of the psychology of religion.

A: Well of course I'd have to give a whole new lecture on that, but the easiest part is to tell you something of the origin of my own interest in the psychology of religion. I suppose it started when I was in college and I attended some of the Buchman meetings. Although I never became a member of the movement, I recognized it as the most dynamic religious movement of its day. It has played itself out and is now only a shadow of its former self, but at any rate it had an impact on me. I began to sense what a religious experience was. I had some friends that I felt had benefited from it and I remained curious about this, curious as to what happened to these people. When I happened to find myself at Harvard looking around for something to study, I got hold of people who had been in this movement to see whether this had been good for them or not. That started my interest in the subject. Maybe my study was not particularly subtle in its methodology, but it was systematic. I collected questionnaires, the old favorite method, but I also supplemented this by interviews and talked with people who first came in contact with the movement ten to twenty years before; then, as I said in one of the lectures, about this same time I got interested in reading William James. Also, I was taught by James B. Pratt, although not in the psychology of religion, and I suppose another thing that stirred my interest in this was my teaching of English literature and of being strangely moved by certain passages in English classics which now I can look back on and I can recognize as the utterances of mystics. There's been something within me that has responded to words of this kind. Therefore as I've grown and considered the changes that have come about, I've been curious as to what caused the changes. Starting with an intense interest in conversion, I have been made aware of the fact that there are changes that seem to come from a deeper level of human nature, and these I've identified as mystical experiences. Now I know that I am only a beginner in this field and there's much beyond what I have been able to bring to you in these lectures.

With respect to methodology, certain with personal documents, one can get as close to the thing as he possibly can. Allport has set up certain systematic tests and methods by which one can study even a single document in a systematic way. Of course there are many sophisticated changes that can be rung on this that I just haven't got time to go into now, and of which you yourself, being younger and closer to the scene, probably know better than than I do. But I believe that the scientist must always be alert for new ways, for the refinement of old methods, and be ready to take a journey on the frontier of science. I, myself, have not been so much impressed by behaviorism in this field; I've turned away from it, just as Maslow did. But I could be wrong there because I know that B. F. Skinner has some very fertile ideas. It is just that he has not interested and impressed me as have James, Pratt, Allport, Maslow, Otto, Stace, and Jung, all of whom have taken religion more seriously than Skinner and have seen more deeply into its nature.

REFERENCES

Cohen, S.: LSD: Side effects and complications. Journal of Nervous and Mental Disease, 1960, Vol. 130, 30-40.

Dishotsky, N. I.: *et al.* LSD and genetic damage. Science, 1971, 172, 430-43.

McCurdy, Harold G.: The personal world. New York, Harcourt, 1961.

INDEX

A

Acceptance and Rejection: 92, 102
Alcoholics Anonymous: 48, 67 ff., 141 ff.
Allegro, John: 142
Allport, Gordon: 16, 82, 113, 145
Alpert, Richard: 55
Anabaptists: 5
Animism: 92, 95, 96, 101, 102, 105, 106
Awakening, Great (Tonga and Fiji): 104 ff.
Awe, sense of: 93; *see also* Otto, Rudolph

B

Baba Ram Dass: 55, 116
Bakan, David: 88
Baptism: 100
Barnett, Homer: 99, 100
Barron, Frank: 88
Battle for the Mind: 17, 24, 44
Bax, Clifford: 58
Becoming: 16
Behavorism: 19
Bias, subjective: 93
Blake, William: 35
Boisen, A.: 83
Brotherhood: 97, 105 ff.
Bruner, Jerome S. :79
Buchman, Frank: 5, 25 ff., 48, 144
Buddhism (ist): 13, 24, 29, 36, 43, 50, 106 ff.

C

Calvin, John: 60, 61
Cannabis drugs: 17
Cannibalism: 97, 104
Carlyle, Thomas: 30, 47
Change in culture: 99

in status: 100
Chemical ecstasy: 17 ff., 92, 94, 95, 108
Chemical Ecstasy: 17, 43
Christ, union with: 37
Christian vs. drug experience: 138, 144
Christian mysticism: 69 ff.
Christian psychology: 64 ff.
Christian Church: 60, 93, 104
indigenous: 102
Clark, Walter Houston: ix, 3, 21, 41, 62 ff., 75 ff., 117
rejoinder on commentaries: 110 ff.
Questions & Answers: 129
Coe, George A.: 15
Coercion of religious experience: 86
Communes: 52 ff., 103
Communion: 108
Communist atheist: 21
Confucians: 107
Consensus: 103
Constructs in Religion: 78 ff., 89
development of: 81
Conversion: 5 ff., 24 ff., 43 ff., 70
Hindu style, 71
demonstration of: 101
nature of: 98-105
group: 101 fn., 104
process of: 98, 101
sociopsychological phenomenon: 103
preconversion phenomena: 92
controlled conversion: 115
Conversion shock: 27
Counter-conversion: 94
Counter-culture: 93, 102
Cox, Harvey: 12
Cross-cultural situations: 92 - 109
Cults, resurrection: 96-97
"Cult of Privacy": 7

D

Daane, James: x, 60, 110, 117 ff., 124

147

Nirvana: 37, 105
Nonrational in religious Experiences: 8, 21 ff.
Normalities and Abnormalities: 108

O

Object of religious experience: 61, 65-73
O'Donnell, Bishop Cletus: 55
Oedipal problems: 37
Organization: 93
Otto, Rudolf: 3, 9 ff, 31, 134, 136: *see* Holy
Oxford Group: 25, 49, 111

P

Pahnke, Walter N.: 18, 36, 50, 79, 80, 87, 113, 143
Participant Observation: 92
Participation, group, multi-individual: 109
Pascal: 50
Paul: 5, 25, 28, 30, 43, 108, 134
Peace: 97, 105, 106, 107
Pentecostalism: 35, 47, 84, 85, 93, 94, 141 ff.
Perception: 79, 82
Personal World, 137
Permanence: 82
Personality, Integrated or Disintegration: 99, 108
Peyote: 95, 96, 108, 116, 120
Pfister, Oscar: 83
Phenomena of religious experience: 21
Phenomenology of worship: 92, 117
Piaget, Jean: 82
Pietism: 5
Pioniyo (Peyote Spirit): 96
Plato: 23, 28, 50
Politics of Experience: 142
Pratt, James B.: 15, 144
Prayer: 95, 108
Prophecy, Jewish: 6
Pruyser, Paul: 16, 87
Psilocybin: 18, 19, 44
Psychedelics: 18 ff., 53, 111, 116, 120, 132, 140
Psychiatric Research Institute of Prague: 37

Psychology and Theology: 60 ff.
Psychological immediacy and unity: 75
Psychology of Religions: 15, 16, 27
Psychotherapists, training of: vii

R

Ramakrishna, Sri: 24
Rankian Symbolism: 37
Rational and Non-Rational: 9 ff.; *see* Experience
Reason in religion: 9, 72
Rebirth, Psychological: 96, 97
Recombination Theory: 99, 100, 103
Rededication: 104
Rejuctionism: 21 ff., 93
Religion as rational and irrational: 9 ff., 72, 78
    constructs in: 78
    uniqueness: 11 ff.
    as mysticism: 66
    Religion and Psychology: 63-65
Religious Consciousness: 15
Religious Experience:
    neglected: 3, 6, 7
    study of: 14 ff., 21 ff.
    ecstasy: 23, 72
    exclusive and inclusive: 77
    induced: 86
    influence of: 41 ff.
    durability of: 105
    manipulated: 95, 98
    self-induced: 95
Republic, Plato's: 24, 50, 57
Reservations: 94-98
Revitalization: 104, 105
Revivalism: 25
Revivals: Christian Endeavor: 105
Revolutions, five: 56
Rubenstein, Richard: 89
Russell, Bertrand: 133 ff.

S

Sagas: 82
St. Anthony: 5, 35
St. Augustine: 26, 46, 103
St. Francis: 23, 35, 50, 56
St. Ignatius: 23, 35
St. Teresa: 23, 33